'Jamal's neutral, yet gently perceptive style allows the stories of her women to shine through, illuminating the myriad points of intersection with Islam in ordinary life. An absolutely fascinating and illuminating read; a book that teaches without lecturing.'
Annabel Crabb, ABC writer and broadcaster

'*Headstrong Daughters* is a thoughtful, honest and compelling window into a community so often talked over or assumed about, but rarely engaged with. Insightful without sugar-coating, this book is a welcome, nuanced portrayal of Australian Muslim women and their varied lives that is desperately needed today. I finished it in a single sitting.'
Susan Carland, author of *Fighting Hislam*

HEADSTRONG DAUGHTERS

Also by Nadia Jamal

The Glory Garage: Growing up Lebanese Muslim in Australia
by Nadia Jamal and Taghred Chandab (2005)

HEADSTRONG DAUGHTERS

Inspiring stories from the new generation
of Australian Muslim women

Nadia Jamal

ALLEN&UNWIN
SYDNEY·MELBOURNE·AUCKLAND·LONDON

Allen & Unwin
83 Alexander Street
Crows Nest NSW 2065
Australia
Phone: (61 2) 8425 0100
Email: info@allenandunwin.com
Web: www.allenandunwin.com

 A catalogue record for this book is available from the National Library of Australia

ISBN 978 1 76029 331 4

Internal design by Midland Typesetters, Australia
Set in 12.75/17.5 pt Dante MT by Midland Typesetters, Australia
Printed and bound in Australia by Griffin Press

10 9 8 7 6 5 4 3 2 1

To my beloved mum,
Hanan Jamal.

5 February 1958 – 15 February 2018

Contents

Author's note

The stories in this book are based on my interviews with Muslim women in the community around Australia. They reflect the issues and concerns these women experience in their daily lives, and their understanding of religious principles and traditions. Some of the practices and attitudes draw on cultural traditions and interpretations rather actual religious teachings. I have included brief explanations where I felt it would be helpful for non-Muslim readers, and I encourage readers to seek further information on Islam from authoritative sources. Any other opinions or interpretations are my own.

Introduction

The first word revealed in the Muslim holy book, the Quran, is *Iqra*. And if you are into revelations, it is the Arabic word for 'read', a command for Muslims that was written over 1400 years ago.

This expression of the importance of learning is directed at all Muslims equally—yes, women included. Judging by the frequent negative stories about the treatment of some Muslim women, I can understand why some people would be surprised to learn that when it comes to women's rights, Islam cemented this sentiment about reading by giving women the right to an education all those hundreds of years ago. Until quite recently, women in Western societies have largely been excluded from formal education.

But those 1400 or so years ago, Islam did not stop there: it gave women other rights that were ahead of the times. Women could own property, seek a divorce and vote. While it is fair to reference these long-held female rights as part of how Islam improved the status of women, I have never found it safe to assume that these rights are actually part of the modern reality of many Muslim women.

Indeed, today, women in Muslim (or Muslim-majority) countries have traditionally been more disadvantaged than their counterparts in the West, who are able to rely on convention, legislation and institutions for what are now mostly regarded as basic human rights.

Twelve years ago, I co-wrote *The Glory Garage*, about the challenges of straddling two different cultures faced by teenaged Australian Muslim girls with Lebanese backgrounds in western Sydney. This is the world in which I was raised. The girls who appeared in this book have since grown up. In *Headstrong Daughters*, most of the women are second generation Australians who are working, married, mothers, and from wider cultural backgrounds including Iraq, Bangladesh and Somalia. Yet they are still Australian women who continue to deal with the challenges of being active members of a broader community while staying true to their faith.

Islam's call to knowledge is one of the defining features of the women portrayed in this book, as they—with the support of their families—have embraced higher learning. Most are university graduates, and some are the first in their family to be so. It is through this education that they have been able to lift their lives as the children of migrants, sometimes overcoming many religious and cultural challenges as part of their journey.

Take 30-year-old Mehal, who completed a PhD at 28, a significant achievement by anyone's measure. She also happens to wear the hijab, the Muslim head covering, and was spat upon by a stranger on her way to the train station from university. I was angry for her as she recounted this story, but as much as I tried to get a reaction out of her, Mehal was able to rise above the attack, determined that she was not going to let this stranger—or my outrage on her behalf—distract her from her goals.

Then there's Amna, who founded an all-female, and mostly Muslim, AFL team in her twenties, recruiting members so as to encourage Muslim women's participation in sport. She had to overcome resistance from her father to go to university, and had to deal with the same kind of negativity about working in the community to get Muslim women to take part in a public sport.

For Nasreen, going to university to improve her life, and that of her child, came out of necessity after she became a young widow and spent several months at home observing a religiously-prescribed mourning period for Muslim women.

These stories highlight that Islam is not practised in a vacuum—Muslims need to go about their daily lives in much the same way as everyone else. However, a lack of understanding about the complexities of Islam and its ethnic, cultural and geographic diversity prevails. Indeed, the largest Muslim country in the world is Indonesia, on Australia's doorstep. And just as not all Muslims are Middle Eastern, not everyone follows the dogmas of their faith.

Unlike a lot of books written about Islam, this book offers the perspective of insiders. I hope these chapters about Australian Muslim female life will both challenge Muslims and inform non-Muslims. I was attracted to the stories because I was forced to ask myself: as a professional woman, could I stay home to mourn a husband for four months and ten days? What would I do if told I couldn't attend a burial for a loved one because I'm a woman? How would I feel as a guest about sitting in a suburban living room deemed a female-only zone?

These narratives were written against the backdrop of recent controversial topics in the headlines about Muslims in Australia: young male high-school students not shaking hands with women; the wearing of the face-covering *niqab* in public; and gender segregation at public events. I first wrote about these issues many years ago, when I was a senior journalist with the *Sydney Morning Herald*. That they are topics debated as something new speaks volumes about how little the national conversation surrounding Australian Muslims has progressed, and where it stands today.

Some of the language used in the public domain about religion in general, or its followers, can be upsetting. A blog on a reputable Australian news website about the Emmys in September 2017 said of the odds of Elisabeth Moss winning the Best Actress award: 'Pretty good, you'd have to think. And she deserves it. Even if she is a Scientologist.' I found the tone of this comment on her religion, if it is her religion, very offensive. Why should her religious beliefs come into it?

Writing about religion is not for the faint-hearted, especially when you are challenging mindsets within your own community as well as outside it. I have found this to be even more the case when, like me, you do not wear a hijab and are not an Islamic scholar. For example, once, after writing several newspaper comment pieces that challenged the Australian Muslim community's views on issues such as segregated community events, a friend's mother stopped her car as I walked home to tell me that she had heard (yes, *heard*) that I was writing negative things about Muslims.

It is with these sensitivities in mind that some of the names and personal details of the subjects in this book have been changed to maintain anonymity.

A big lesson I learned in my former career as a journalist was that getting *a* story didn't mean that I had *the* story. This collection of vignettes is *not* the full story of Muslim women in Australia. It is simply one contribution to the complex multicultural story of Australia—it seeks to draw open the curtain a little further on how some important religious doctrines are being applied in the daily lives of Muslims.

Being a Muslim means that you always know where you stand. At least, that's what Muslims are taught from a young age—that Islam has the answers to all of life's dilemmas. This is because Islam is a way of life, with the Quran and related texts used as guides for how you should live. Religion therefore is a part of a Muslim's life from the moment they open their eyes in the morning—we are expected to recite in our heads a few words of gratitude to Allah for being given another day on Earth—to every step thereafter until your head hits the pillow again and you recite more words that remember God.

But any relationship—familial, romantic or professional—has its challenges and the same is true of your relationship with faith. Our intellect and emotions will inevitably have an impact on how it is lived.

For instance, I find Ramadan a real slog. My family finds my negative views about it disappointing, as it's one of the five compulsory pillars of Islam. In my family, it's expected that fasting gets easier the older you get, but that has not been my experience. So when I think about my thirteen-year-old nephew, Majid, committing to it, it puts me to shame that, at 42, I'm looking for reasons to get out of doing it.

I find it hard to get excited about the pronouncements from those around me that Ramadan will soon be upon the world's Muslims. I find myself wondering why Ramadan seems to be the one date on the calendar that always comes around so quickly. A spiritual awakening. A spiritual journey. A spiritual purification. These are just a few of the many uplifting phrases used to describe Ramadan that, in the modern world, spread like wildfire on social media posts.

Yet, there are other sides to Ramadan that are little discussed. Bad breath is one of them. Then there's the interrupted sleep from the need to make frequent trips to the bathroom because, having been unable to consume any liquid during the day as part of the fast, you've guzzled large amounts of it after the sun's gone down. There's also *suhur*, which takes place before daybreak and is a kind of light breakfast that Muslims wake for at about 4 a.m. each day during Ramadan. I drag myself to the table, bleary-eyed and grumpy because I can never be sure I'll be able to get back to sleep before the alarm goes off again for work.

Ramadan also brings for me the recollection of past indiscretions, such as when in primary school I once (okay, maybe twice) secretly broke my fast on a bag of chips while hiding in a far-flung corner of the playground. I then went home as if nothing had happened and luckily didn't get put through the 'show me your tongue' test by my mum, Hanan. (Never eat Twisties, Cheezels or Cheeseballs, because the yellow stain will take ages to wear off.)

Is Islam a religion that is perfectly executed every day by its peaceful followers in the world? No. Do these adherents make mistakes in life, like everyone else? Yes. Do Muslims sometimes feel conflicted about some elements of their own faith, but choose not to give up on it? Of course. Islam recognises that once a person seeks knowledge, they will inevitably be challenged—sometimes in a good way, sometimes not. But that's the point, because it's about being personally tested and overcoming these hardships.

For me, the challenge of Ramadan is a strong metaphor for other things going on in my life. When a friend's young daughter once complained about how long it was taking us to walk to the beach, he advised her to enjoy the journey because life isn't always about the destination. I for one know that I would be a better Muslim if I applied this advice not only to my fasting, but to other experiences and activities too—like reading.

1

Bridging the divide

'What's it like?'

Ola is getting used to being asked this question about her husband, Abdul, who is a Muslim like her—but from the Sunni branch, not the Shia branch of Islam to which she and her family belong.

'What's what like?' she responds.

'Being married to a Sunni?' her questioner, a fellow Muslim, persists.

Growing up in Australia, Ola, who comes from a Lebanese background, cannot recall experiencing the level of prejudice about the different Muslim branches that confronts her almost daily now. Even in high school—in a part of Sydney where she was surrounded by a large Muslim population—she was never asked to explain what sort of a Muslim she was, what it was like being a Shia or what the difference was between Shias and Sunnis.

This is likely because Ola's parents' generation grew up in the Middle East during the era following the collapse of the Ottoman Empire, reportedly a period of relative truce between the two branches as they came to grips with European colonialism, which was perceived by some as a threat. Traditionally, Sunnis have been the more dominant of the two groups.

In recent times, however, some of the balance of political power has shifted from Sunnis to Shias. Some commentators cite the war in Iraq in 2003 as creating this modern change, when the reportedly majority Shia population—once persecuted under Saddam Hussein, a Sunni—took much of the political control. As sectarian war continues in Iraq today, Sunnis and Shias routinely kill each other.

Against this backdrop of tension, Ola is acutely aware how much times have changed since her school days—and not for the better. Even her children have recently had her Shia background thrown in their faces.

The difference between Sunnis and Shias is an ancient one and can be summed up in the following way: Sunnis chose the closest supporter (and father-in-law) of the Prophet Muhammad—Abu Bakr—as his first successor, or *caliph*, to lead Muslims in the seventh century. Not long afterwards, Shias threw their support behind Ali ibn Abi Talib (or Imam Ali), who was the Prophet's son-in-law and cousin, and therefore his kinsman. It could be argued that one group chose a somewhat democratic route to leadership, while the other pursued a dynastic version where one's position is inherited and 'divinely' anointed.

Imam Ali was eventually chosen as the fourth *caliph* to lead the *Ummah*, the Muslim community around the world, but not before there was considerable violence. Ultimately, his assassination led to the break-up of Muslims into two branches that have rarely united since.

Sunni Muslims have traditionally been the largest group within Islam, and Shias the second largest, although they comprise the majority Muslim population in some countries, including Iran. Over the centuries, these two branches have developed their own very distinct schools of thought, social mores and religious practices.

Worldwide modern states seek to promote inter-faith dialogue between the major religions—Christians, Muslims and Jews. Yet in modern times, it is Muslims—who say they believe in the same God and are brought up to believe that all Muslims are brothers and sisters in Islam—who seem to be most publicly at loggerheads.

The irony of this is not lost on Ola.

Asked how she met her husband, Abdul, Ola laughs and says it was a simple case of 'love thy neighbour'. When she was fifteen, she lived with her mother and younger sister in a townhouse; Abdul and his family, who also came from a Lebanese background, moved into the same complex.

Her mother, Nouha, was the first to notice Abdul. 'You should see the boy next door,' she happily announced after arriving home one day.

Ola soon had a chance to judge for herself. She ran into Abdul in the complex carpark and came to the same conclusion as her mother: Abdul was indeed good looking. This made her extremely nervous around him and Ola barely exchanged two words with him for the first six months after he moved in.

Abdul was five years older and drove a red sports car with an exhaust that could be heard a kilometre away. Secretly, Ola enjoyed the roar of the car, as it alerted her to when Abdul was going out and when he returned. This advance warning meant that she could get into position near a window to catch a glimpse of him without giving herself away.

Ola's younger sister Safa, then twelve, regularly bumped into Abdul outside. He started to look out for her and would ask if she or her mother needed anything. He was aware that there was no man living at her house and had worked out that her parents were not together.

After a few months, Abdul felt comfortable enough to ask Safa to tell her 'stranger' sister, Ola, to say hello the next time they bumped into each other. Safa excitedly passed on the message as soon as she got home, but Ola dismissed it. Even at that early stage, she knew she liked Abdul, but she was too scared to get involved and continued to avoid him.

A few weeks later, her sister came home carrying a small piece of paper. She shoved it straight into Ola's hand. It had Abdul's mobile number scribbled on it.

Ola now had to make a decision. She eventually worked up the courage to call Abdul, and soon afterwards, they met at a cafe.

Although Ola grew up unaffected by the differences between Muslims and Abdul being Sunni did not worry her, she was still aware of the politics of the situation and decided to ask him about it at their first meeting.

'Is it going to be a problem?' Ola asked straight out.

'What do you mean?' Abdul looked across at her, genuinely puzzled.

'For when we get married,' Ola replied matter-of-factly.

'Whoa . . .' Abdul blurted, leaning away from the table.

Ola was undeterred: 'Is it going to be a problem with your parents that I'm Shia?'

Abdul threw up his arms and confided he didn't know much about the issue. 'What's Shia?' he asked innocently.

Ola proceeded to explain some of the major differences between Shias and Sunnis.

There was nothing in all this that disturbed Abdul, and when she thinks back to this moment, Ola realises just how unjudgmental Abdul was—a quality he has maintained. The pair continued to secretly see each other for a year before Ola's mother pulled her aside and asked about Abdul's intentions. Nouha had suspected for a while that Ola and Abdul were together, but as long as they were discreet, she trusted that her daughter would not cross any boundaries.

Abdul had confided in his parents about his feelings towards Ola. So when his mother approached Nouha about the families meeting to discuss a future between the two young people, Ola was confident that things between her and Abdul would soon become official.

Ola's parents had been divorced for a while, but she was still close to her father, who had once talked her out of getting engaged to a Turkish-Australian Muslim man. When her mother gave her father the heads-up about Abdul being a Sunni from a Lebanese-Australian family, Nouha's spin on it was to ask him rhetorically: 'Which would you prefer for your daughter: a Turk who doesn't speak a word of Arabic; or Sunni who does?'

For Nouha, Abdul's Sunni background was never a problem. She was not conservative at all when it came to religion, a stance that especially suited Ola on this occasion. Besides, Ola was convinced that her family would recognise that Abdul was from a good family, and that this would win out.

Twelve years later, Ola and Abdul are still together and have three daughters.

'No one in our families has ever made us feel that we are not one of them,' Ola maintains, although she does recall that her father-in-law tested her patience on one occasion in the early days of her marriage, when he made an off-the-cuff comment about her praying on a rock at home.

This is a jibe she says Sunnis regularly make about Shias. For Shias, using a stone (or *turbah*) for performing their prayers (*salat*) is obligatory because it symbolises praying directly on the earth. For Sunnis, the practice is considered taboo as it promotes the notion of idolatry.

Ola has used the same *turbah* for prayers for many years. The piece of clay is in the form of a tablet and about the size of a 50-cent coin. Many such tablets have been brought back to Australia from Karbala in Iraq, where Imam Hussein—Imam Ali's son and a grandson of the Prophet—was killed. Before his death, some argue, the schism between the branches of Islam was political; afterwards, it became more overtly religious.

As she prostrates during her prayers, which are performed five times a day by Muslims, Ola places her forehead on the tablet. While these tablets usually carry inscriptions that invoke revered figures for Shias, Ola has chosen to delicately scrape hers clean as she prefers not to have any image between her and God when she prays.

When she prostrates on the tablet, Ola believes that she is performing her ritual on pure earth. In the days of the Prophet, followers did not pray on carpets as is the common practice today; soil was considered a clean place to do so. Soil then became a sign of cleanliness, and the *turbah* is considered a token of this philosophy.

An extension of this idea is that, under extreme circumstances, earth can be used as a substitute for a Muslim who is performing *wudu* (ablution) for their prayers and cannot access clean water, a problem that can particularly arise in desert communities. Cleanliness is an important requirement in Islam—the proverb of cleanliness being next to Godliness has much resonance. Muslims are expected to wash themselves clean before each prayer session, when hygiene has not been maintained. This involves washing the parts of the body that are generally exposed, including ones' face and feet, in a certain way. The same cleanliness is expected of the location where they pray.

As Imam Hussein had an important relationship with the Prophet, the soil from Karbala is considered a sacred place to pray for Shias. For Ola, having a piece of that soil in the form of a tablet in her Sydney home is the next best thing to praying in Karbala.

Unlike Shias, Sunnis reject the use of a *turbah*, arguing that the Prophet never carried one and therefore its use is an unsubstantiated change to the faith. Instead, Sunnis allow their heads to directly touch the floor during prayers.

Ola is not wedded to the notion of always praying with the *turbah*. When she visits a mosque that Abdul favours and is frequented by Sunnis, she chooses not to carry it with her and is comfortable enough to perform her prayers without it on occasion. Mosques are likely to be divided along branch lines, with these centres of prayer informally designated as Sunni or Shia depending on their location, financial backers and the background of the imams who lead the prayer sessions.

While she can pray without it, Ola continues to feel strongly about her 'rock', as it is a constant reminder of the earth that humans have been created from and the earth to which they will return.

In some London circles, the children of Sunni–Shia marriages are reportedly referred to as 'Su–Shi'. While it is not an expression that Ola is familiar with, she wishes Muslims would put their prejudices aside for the sake of her children's generation.

She was distressed when her eldest daughter, Sabrine, confided that a young cousin from Abdul's side of the family had teased her at a family event about her mother being different to other mothers.

'This was the day I had been dreading,' Ola explains, 'I don't want my children to feel strange about me. I don't think it should matter that her father and I are from different branches, but with everything that's happening in the world . . . it does matter.'

The young cousin had pointed out to Sabrine that Ola prays differently to the rest of the Sunni family, with her hands alongside her body rather than folded at her chest.

'My children have never understood anything else,' Ola says. 'I told my daughter to remember that we are all Muslim, but that there are certain things that I do differently to her dad and it's nothing that's going to affect her life.'

Ola hopes to guide her children so that they do not feel any less Muslim because she is Shia.

'We believe in the same God,' she says of Muslims, 'the same holy book, the same holy sites, the same Prophets . . . Abdul and I are more similar than different, the biggest similarity being that we are both Muslim.'

And Ola wants to teach her children not to generalise about others based on their religion. 'We will see what the future holds for our kids. I hope it gets better. I'm doing what I can. It starts in my household—respecting all religious people. We should be an example to other Muslims.'

She hopes to have done enough so that if her children are ever asked whether they are Sunni or Shia, they will be sufficiently informed to respond: 'I'm Muslim.'

But she is also realistic about the personal challenges that come with being in such a relationship with Abdul. On a day-to-day level, there are some obvious differences in the way she practises her faith versus how Abdul does things, particularly when it comes to fasting during the holy month of Ramadan, when Muslims abstain from eating and drinking between sunrise and sunset.

During Ramadan, Ola waits until the last rays of light have disappeared from the sky and it is dark outside to break her fast. For Sunnis, the fast is broken when the sun is no longer visible on the horizon, so there may still be sunlight. Since this means that Ola breaks her fast later during Ramadan, if she is sharing the table with Abdul's family, they sometimes joke about when she will start eating: 'Are you going to wait for the stars to come out?'

Other differences include that Sunnis perform extra prayers, called *Tarawih*, at night during Ramadan; Shias commemorate *Ashura*, a day of mourning for a martyr, held during the first month of the Islamic calendar.

Ola insists that Abdul is supportive of her position. Knowing this helps her navigate these differences when she is around his family. 'If it doesn't bother him, then it shouldn't matter to anyone else when I break my fast—or how I pray.'

In some parts of Sydney, though, the attitude among Sunnis and Shias towards one another is on a whole different level. There have been news reports in the past few years of Shias being targeted by other Muslims as the conflicts in Iraq and Syria rage.

Ola explains that some suburbs are informally segregated (socially, religiously and politically) along Muslim branch lines, with the Canterbury-Bankstown area considered more a Sunni area, while the suburbs that make up the St George area are more predominantly home to Shias.

An example of how this divide plays out occurred when Abdul visited a pizza shop in Arncliffe, in the St George zone. While he waited for his meal, he was asked by the shop owner where he lived; Abdul replied Bankstown.

'So you're a Sunni,' the man concluded.

'Yeah, but I'm married to a Shia girl and you probably know her father,' Abdul added, trying to find common ground.

Certain names can also quickly identify the Muslim branch to which an individual belongs, as each group attempts to honour the key figures in Islam who support their views of succession following the Prophet's death. The names Ali, Hussein and Hassan are especially common among Shias, while Abu Bakr and Omar are generally considered to be Sunni names. This is not to say that these names are not shared between the branches, as Muslims are encouraged to give their children Arabic/Muslim names generally.

Furthermore, despite the enmity that is being played out in some parts of the world between the two branches, it is noteworthy that the groups are not formally divided when they travel to Mecca in Saudi Arabia for the annual Hajj pilgrimage. At Islam's holiest sites, the two come together to fulfil their important religious obligation at the same time. While there are anecdotal reports that the groups informally separate at some of the different locations they must visit during Hajj, officially no separate lines or queues exist for pilgrims from the different branches.

However, Ola tells of one disappointing incident at Hajj involving her grandmother, Soumaya, who first completed the pilgrimage as a nineteen year old. Now 81, Soumaya has made a total of nineteen trips to Hajj. Most Muslims perform the duty only once in their lifetime, as is the requirement, so Soumaya is a serious overachiever in this regard.

During one of her pilgrimages, Ola says her grandmother was refused service in a shop because the owner had noticed a small tattoo of a sword (*sayf*) on her right hand. As a little girl growing up in Palestine, Soumaya had begged her mother to allow one of the local women to give her the tattoo, which represents Imam Ali's sword, believed to have been given to him by the Prophet.

'This kind of thing happens there?' Ola asked when she heard her grandmother's story. 'Isn't it meant to be a holy place?'

Even without such a tattoo, Ola explains how Muslims can often tell the difference between a Shia and a Sunni just by looking at them. She observes, for instance, that Shia women are generally identifiable by the placement of their hijab closer to their eyes and a preference for dark-coloured clothing. Sunni women, meanwhile, are sometimes regarded as not as conservative with their garb and prone to choosing more colourful hijabs, and wearing them more loosely.

Ola is aware that not everyone involved in a Sunni–Shia relationship has the same mostly positive journey. She has heard stories of intermarried couples who have struggled to gain the acceptance of their families because they are judged as going against their values.

While she has never been asked to 'convert' to Sunnism, anecdotally this is something that some Shias end up doing to appease their partner. And Ola has also observed that Sunni parents tend to be more against the idea of their children marrying into the other branch of Islam, while Shia families are more accepting.

One such story that became common knowledge was Layla's, who came from a well-known Sunni family and waited about ten years for her parents to agree to her marrying a Shia. One of her three older brothers strongly opposed her marriage to Hassan. This brother had a significant influence on her parents and regularly threatened to disown Layla, and have them do the same.

Layla sat tight for many years, hoping her family's views would soften over time. She had been raised to believe that all Muslims are equal, so the degree of their rejection of Hassan surprised her and she was forced to learn the hard way that, in practice, some Muslims do not really share this sentiment.

As a young woman, Layla hadn't realised that her already limited pool of potential suitors—they had to be Muslim—would be further narrowed to a Muslim from a particular branch.

Hassan, who had been married before, was prepared to wait for however long it took for Layla and her family to come around. Layla loved him, but she was extremely loyal to her parents, at times more so than she was towards Hassan. Sometimes, when things got tough between them, she would urge him to move on with another woman. She could not do what other girls had done if they could not get their families on-side—that is, run-off with a man—because she was brought up to believe that this would ruin her family's reputation.

It is hard to believe now, but Layla put her personal life with Hassan on hold for all those years, hoping her parents would eventually agree to the marriage. All she ever wanted was to do things the right way, or at least her parents' version of it. Without her parents' *ridah* (approval), she feared that she would be entering the marriage on the wrong footing and be forever cursed.

Layla's parents relied on their adult sons and were scared of their reaction. In this respect, their lives were ruled by the emotions of these men. This hold that sons can have on a household occurs a lot in Arab families.

While her parents worried about the familial repercussions of Layla marrying in secret, after so much time they could no longer give her a valid reason as to why she should not be able to marry Hassan.

As Hassan had waited so long for Layla, her parents did not need any more proof of his commitment. Layla, for her part, knew that if she continued to wait, she could jeopardise her chance of motherhood. She was 38 and needed to make a move soon to ensure that her dream of having a family could be fulfilled. Over time, this had become obvious to her parents, too.

Layla and Hassan eventually married, signing their marriage contract at the office of a sheikh—a Muslim religious leader/scholar—with her parents' blessing. Only a handful of people were told it was happening as Layla and her parents worried that her brothers would ruin things. Consequently, Layla was denied the chance of having a big white wedding. It was simply a case of packing her bags and moving in with Hassan after their visit to the sheikh.

Meanwhile, the most outspoken brother continues to proclaim, both at home and in public, that Shias are not 'real' Muslims. This, even though he now has a brother-in-law who is one.

Ola is confident about her religious identity, and believes her relationship with Abdul is an example to others.

'It's dumb that people dwell on things that happened a million years ago,' she says of how the divisions in Islam are currently playing out. 'It's not something that's going to stop me from loving my husband.'

She smiles as she recounts how Abdul teases her when they are out with their friends about how she proposed to him on their first date.

In public, she dismisses Abdul's interpretation of the events of that day. But when they are alone together, Ola is not shy to admit to him: 'I'm so glad your family moved into that townhouse.'

2

The single female pilgrim

After her beloved grandmother died, Zara, whose family came to Australia from Lebanon, became more interested in religion.

'If you had known me as a teenager, you would never have guessed that I would end up wearing the hijab,' she explains. She recalls a conversation that she had at fifteen with a family friend.

'When's it going to be your turn?' he asked, about taking on the hijab.

'Never,' Zara was adamant.

'Never say never ... say *Inshallah* [God willing],' he counselled.

But this only added to Zara's defiance: 'No, I won't!'

A few years earlier, Zara had expressed the opposite sentiment. Her mother had stopped at a local newsagency near their home to run an errand when the woman serving her began asking questions about her hijab. After her mother explained its significance and paid for her items, the woman looked over to Zara, who was lingering behind her mother, and said, 'I hope you never put that on like your mum.'

Zara was shocked by the woman's comment, and bluntly responded, 'I am going to.'

Although she was young, Zara looked up to her mother and was not swayed by the woman's passive-aggressive behaviour. When she reflects on that encounter now, Zara thinks it was more about a little girl wanting to defend her mother than really understanding what was going on.

Zara's views about the hijab have since come full circle.

At nineteen, not long after her grandmother's death, she made the formal decision to wear the hijab and began to attend regular religion classes with other Muslim women keen to develop their understanding of their faith. Led by an *ustatha* (female teacher), Zara was one of hundreds of women who passed through this tutor's door in search of a deeper connection with the religious texts.

Zara continued to attend the *ustatha*'s classes throughout her twenties and into her early thirties. It was after one of these classes that Zara's friend Hanan had some news to share. 'Zara, I'm going to Hajj and . . . I want you to come with me.'

Zara felt that she was being put on the spot. 'Who are you going with?' she questioned Hanan. 'You don't have a husband.'

'I'm going with an all-girls group with the *ustatha*. There's actually some leeway for single women like us.'

Until this point, Zara had imagined she would undertake Hajj to Mecca with a husband. They would stand together on Mount Arafat, where the Prophet Muhammad is believed to have delivered his final sermon. Like many women, she assumed she would get married in her twenties, have children in her thirties and later in life, when her children were older and could manage without her, she and her husband would have the time and money to travel and fulfil the pilgrimage. Yet she was still single, for the same reason as many others her age—she hadn't yet met a person she wanted to marry.

Zara's assumed timeline for Hajj reflected the experiences of her parents, married sisters and family friends. However, she had recently noticed a shift in expectations about Hajj: while once Muslims would wait until they were much older to perform the compulsory ritual, increasingly the younger generation—spurred to become highly educated about Islam by the significant amount of negative news about their religion—are making the trip and committing to all the responsibilities that come with being a pilgrim.

Completing the Hajj pilgrimage is one of the five pillars of Islam: it must be conducted at least once in a Muslim's lifetime if they have the physical and financial capability to do it. The practicalities of visiting Mecca are similar to the planning that goes into any overseas trip: who's going? How much will it cost? How much time off work can one take?

But there is a major difference between how Muslim men and women perform Hajj: a woman cannot make the pilgrimage on her own if she is young and single. Muslim women who travel to Mecca must do so with a *mahram*—either their husband or a Muslim man who can act as a protector or guardian. This includes a father, brother or father-in-law. If a woman does not have a *mahram*, then Hajj is not obligatory. For their part, male pilgrims are not expected to have a *mahram*.

Many Muslim scholars have argued that at its essence, the *mahram* rule is about the protection of women, both from the perspective of a safe journey and her moral character. In its implementation in modern times, however, there is concern that it is a means of controlling women and their ability to move freely. In some Muslim countries, women, regardless of their age or marital status, are forbidden from travelling or going on excursions alone, even for a short time, if they are not accompanied by a *mahram*; this extends to activities such as booking a hotel room, which a single woman would be unable to do on her own. A few years ago, Saudi officials turned back more than a thousand female pilgrims from Nigeria because they were not accompanied by *mahrams*.

At the time, the Saudis said their law requires each female pilgrim under the age of 45 to have a male sponsor during the journey.

The *mahram* rule on Hajj was not something to which Zara had previously given much thought. This changed after her chat with Hanan, as it was starting to dawn on her that being a single Muslim woman brought with it some complexities she had not previously considered.

Zara's parents, like many migrants to Australia, strongly valued education and encouraged her to go to university. She had grown up knowing that she had every opportunity in the world and eventually secured a well-paid job in marketing.

But when Zara next returned to work after the conversation with Hanan, she found it hard to focus. Most days she felt compelled to stay back to keep up with her workload, and she was finding it increasingly difficult to hide just how disillusioned she was becoming with her job.

If Zara had been asked to describe her boss, Michael, the word 'difficult' would have been at the top of her list, as would his propensity to explode on the smallest pretext ('f*ck off' was one of his favourite expressions). He was the product of another era, but somehow—and Zara shook her head in disbelief at this—he managed to hold on to his senior post in an age of HR departments and conduct policies.

Meanwhile, Hanan was not giving up on the idea of Zara travelling with her. 'Come with me,' she would repeat when they met up at religion class.

'I'm not ready,' Zara would usually insist, although one time, she snapped at Hanan: 'Stop asking me. When I go, it will be with my husband.'

But the more Zara struggled with her work, the more she thought about Hanan's proposal and the more attractive it became. Most people in her position who needed some time out would typically turn to exercise, a spa or an overseas holiday. But the Hajj seed had been well and truly planted, and there was no way to take it back.

One night when she arrived home from work and collapsed into bed from exhaustion, Zara knew it was time to make a change. 'I need to do something. I can't continue like this,' she berated herself.

Zara started to think that Hajj might be the answer to her problems. She knew she needed to spend more time on her spirituality, and she didn't feel that she could do that with work being the way it was.

By then, Ramadan was approaching and in the Islamic calendar, the month for Hajj falls a couple of months after the end of Ramadan.

Zara finally called Hanan: 'I might do this.'

With these words, her life took a whole new direction.

It was Sunday morning, the one day of the week when Zara always sat down with her parents for breakfast. Her mother put on a big spread.

Before she had even properly taken her seat, Zara blurted: 'Guess what? I'm going to Hajj this year.'

Zara's parents were always supportive of her decisions, and this time was no different. Both her parents had already completed the pilgrimage. Her mother was over 60 when she made the journey for the first time and had been able to go without Zara's father; due to her age and because she was travelling with an organised group she was able to travel without a *mahram*. Her father, now in his seventies, had recently had some health issues and Zara knew that she couldn't expect him to make the trip again with her, especially since he had only completed Hajj the year before and the experience was still so fresh for him.

Zara could have convinced her only brother, Fadi, who was a few years younger, to sign up with her, but he had recently been promoted at work and she feared the trip would interrupt his momentum. Besides, as she would discover herself, the privilege of Hajj comes with a hefty price tag and Zara knew that Fadi was not yet in a position to afford it.

Just because I don't have a husband, Zara thought, *I can't say to my dad and brother, 'Stop whatever it is you're doing and come with me.'*

Unlike her parents, Fadi had some reservations about Zara's plans: 'Are you sure you want to travel there on your own? They [the authorities] might make it hard for you.'

Hajj was not for the faint-hearted, he counselled her. She would be one of the more than two million Muslims who converge on Mecca at the same time from all over the world, from many races and nationalities. While it is said to be a profound display of the unity of Islam, on a day-to-day level Zara would need to navigate the many different cultural experiences and expectations of the various pilgrims with whom she would come into contact. For many pilgrims, this would be the first time they had stepped outside of their country.

Hajj is certainly no walk in the park. Many pilgrims, after they come home, speak of being ill-prepared—not for the spiritual challenge but for the physical demands. The journey begins with a long plane trip to Saudi Arabia, where various prescribed steps must be met over a ten-day period. These involve joining the tide of humanity to circle the *Ka'bah*—the building at the centre of Mecca's mosque—seven times; a bus journey to Mina for the ritual stoning of the devil; standing on Mount Arafat from midday until sunset; taking part in a night prayer; and camping overnight.

Zara would also have to practise considerable patience (not one of her strongest qualities) during Hajj, because the sheer number of worshippers meant there would inevitably be long queues on a scale she had never seen or experienced. Fadi knew that Zara liked her own space, and he was just trying to prepare her for the idea that Hajj was no holiday.

After completing her application form and paying a deposit, Zara realised that her trip—her first overseas—would be more expensive than an average getaway. All up, for accommodation and airfare, the cost would be $11,000, a big chunk of her savings.

Zara was worried that not having a *mahram* during Hajj would become an issue and didn't want to do anything to jeopardise her trip. But ever since Hanan first suggested that she consider the pilgrimage, Zara had begun to hear stories about other women who weren't married and had been able to go. Her head was swirling with questions. What if a woman isn't married, or never marries, and wants to go to Hajj? Is there any situation where she may find herself requiring a male escort in Hajj, and what if one isn't available?

To put her mind at ease, Zara reached out to the *ustatha* who would be leading the group of women with whom Zara would be travelling. She told Zara that in her learned opinion Saudi Arabia's *mahram* rule relating to single women was more a feature of its strict cultural and social policies, as many scholars believed that there was a concession for women to conduct Hajj without a *mahram* if it was their first pilgrimage. As the *ustatha* had visited Saudi Arabia many times with groups of female-only pilgrims, she understood how to navigate the local rules and was confident that they would not be violating them.

'The rule is not there to hinder women,' the *ustatha* stressed, adding that they would travel as an official group, making things easier for all concerned. Zara trusted that those organising the trip knew what they were doing and decided to put her fate in their hands.

She also admired the way the *ustatha*'s mind worked. Born in Australia, the *ustatha* was in her fifties and had studied Arabic. Her understanding of Islamic teachings was extra-ordinarily deep and she had dedicated herself over many years to passing on this knowledge to young Australian women like Zara. The women who attended the *ustatha*'s classes came from all walks of life—stay-at-home mothers, working women and university students.

Hajj participants are encouraged to register for courses to prepare for the journey. Some of the essential topics include: how to make the most out of Hajj; a step-by-step guide to Hajj rites; the spiritual significance of each rite; pictorial presenta-tions of the journey; what to pack and how to pack; and Hajj and women's issues. Like all the religious classes Zara had attended over the years, the Hajj classes were segregated with women in one group and men in another.

Zara made sure she attended the *ustatha*'s special classes to prepare for Hajj. These covered all aspects of the trip, from mundane details, such as the clothing required to meet modesty standards, to practicalities like which hotels they would be staying at. The students went through what was expected of them to fulfil their obligations at each of the holy sites they were scheduled to visit. In the city of Medina, for example, the focus would be on the life of the Prophet Muhammad, as it is known as the Prophet's city. All of those in attendance were provided with a book of specific prayers to learn for Hajj, as these would need to be recited at certain intervals throughout the trip.

While she would travel with a mixed group on the plane from Sydney Airport, once they arrived in Saudi Arabia the men and women would be separated and their passports and accompanying paperwork checked in different queues. She was assured none of the men would be expected to act as Zara's escort when they got to Hajj.

'Having the *ustatha* there will mean that we will have a mountain of knowledge with us,' Hanan promised Zara.

Zara would be leaving for Hajj in four weeks and she had many things to take care of before she got on the plane. A daily theme now was to maintain her commitment to *salat* (prayers) and *du'a* (supplications to Allah). At the top of Zara's *du'as* was to ask Allah to smooth the way for her trip to Mecca and forgive her sins.

Zara did not consider Saudi Arabia to be a modern country, but she was reliably informed that it was no desert; all of life's creature comforts would be on offer. Indeed, in recent times there has been some criticism that the tone at Hajj has changed with the development of five-star accommodation that serve lavish meals. As she was determined to stay true to the essence of Hajj, Zara took a minimalist approach to packing, choosing only those items she knew she really needed. After all, Hajj is meant to be the great equaliser, with no reference to a person's wealth or position in society. This is reinforced by the dress code—all pilgrims wear simple clothing, which makes it hard to distinguish between them. No one is supposed to jump queues, be they a politician or a businessperson.

The planned trip to Hajj had brought to the surface some unresolved issues for Zara. Muslims consider the pilgrimage as part of a cleansing process, which meant that she had to go through a period of introspection. She had to assess her life, including work and relationships, which forced her to consider who and what was important, and to think about the kind of life she wanted to lead.

Lately, her total focus had been on work. Now she wondered if she was in the right job, and how she could make more time for her family. Asking herself these questions, she started to think that maybe she was undeserving to go on Hajj.

As she worked through her issues, Zara grew more anxious

about only sharing her news of Hajj with a few close friends. This would minimise the chance of her lack of a *mahram* becoming gossip fodder and potentially cruelling her trip.

As the pilgrimage drew closer, Zara started to feel more comfortable about things, having gone through various phases of self-reflection. She wasn't as hard on herself as she had been a few weeks earlier, and she began widening the circle of people she told about her impending journey.

Her friends, many of whom were yet to embark on Hajj, started to ask Zara to deliver bespoke *du'as* on their behalf while in Mecca. It was getting harder for Zara to remember all of the requests, so she purchased a small black leather diary and asked her well-wishers to jot them down. 'Iman: Pray for my mum because she has an important doctor's appointment coming up and we hope everything's okay. Dalal: Pray for my brother because he is on the wrong path. Khalil: Pray that I meet a nice woman soon and get married.'

Zara called the book her *du'a* diary. So many people had entrusted their prayers to her, a duty she took very seriously.

Even when her visa for Saudi Arabia was approved, Zara still had a hard time believing that she was actually going to Mecca. Nevertheless, it forced her to work through the logistics, including asking for leave. The trip itself, including time spent travelling to and from her destination, as well as being on the ground in Saudi Arabia for extra prayers, would make three weeks all up. But Zara wanted to take more time off on her return to recover at home and not have to dive straight back into work.

She had worked herself into a state about what Michael would say. As she wasn't giving much notice, Zara convinced herself that she would be better off resigning and looking for another job on her return. Right now, Hajj came first.

Zara knew that she was embarking on a life-changing experience and nothing was going to get in her way. Besides, it was her negative feelings about work that had pushed her onto this path in the first place.

She organised a meeting with Michael. He was hard to pin down, but eventually she got fifteen minutes in his diary. When she finally got to sit down opposite him in his office, Zara did not waste any time.

'Michael, I've decided to resign,' she said firmly.

Michael looked surprised. 'Why? No . . . you can't.'

It was Zara's turn to be taken aback. It was no secret that she had been having a tough time in the office and Michael hadn't taken an interest in helping her to work through it.

Zara explained that she was going on Hajj and she would need to take a substantial amount of time off, and soon.

'You're being dramatic,' Michael reasoned. 'How much time?'

'Five weeks,' Zara quickly responded, and waited for a negative reaction.

'We can do that,' Michael confirmed. 'Take the time you need.'

Before their meeting, Zara had been convinced that her conversation with Michael would be difficult. But not only was Michael supportive of her plans, he came across as genuinely pleased for her and even told Zara that he valued her contributions at work. His positive reaction made her question whether some of the anxiety she had been experiencing recently about her job was unfounded.

Everything happens for a reason, Zara told herself afterwards. If she had confided to Michael earlier how badly she was feeling about work, maybe she wouldn't have started on this journey to Hajj.

Making peace with one's life—including family and friends—is a big part of the spiritual preparation for Hajj, and not just with fellow Muslims, but anyone with whom one's relationship has been tested and is strained. This is why seeking forgiveness is compulsory for pilgrims before setting off for Hajj, as the idea of a pardon goes to the very essence of Hajj as a journey of repentance. A pilgrim returns with their sins forgiven by Allah.

In the days leading up to Hajj, Zara asked everyone she could think of for forgiveness. Her family and close friends acknowledged her request, even though they told her that she did not have anything to be sorry about. But to ensure that she had all bases covered—Zara didn't have time to reach out to everyone individually—she decided to publish a status update on her Facebook page with a general message of forgiveness: 'In case you don't already know . . . I will be undertaking my pilgrimage (Hajj) this year, *Inshallah* [God willing]. If I have ever offended or insulted you, knowingly or otherwise, I would like to apologise and sincerely ask you to forgive me.' She signed it: 'I will remember you on my journey.'

Zara felt especially overwhelmed by the positive feedback from her non-Muslim friends. It represented an opportunity to share information about Islam and Hajj. More than anything, she was genuinely humbled by the warm wishes.

Zara sought to speak to Michael in person again, seeking to ask for his forgiveness, since work and her relationships there had been a big part of her thought processes in the lead-up to Hajj. She had to be content with speaking to him by phone because he was away from the office at a conference.

'Michael, I'm leaving for Hajj soon and I need to talk to you about something . . . about forgiveness,' Zara explained.

She continued: 'I want to ask you for forgiveness, for anything that I have done wrong by you. This is something I need to do before I begin my journey to Saudi Arabia.'

Michael was silent for a few seconds. 'Zara, you have nothing to apologise for. I am the one who should be asking you for forgiveness!'

Was this Michael's way of atoning, Zara wondered? She had never heard him say sorry before, even when he got things wrong. In fact, he had a reputation for being obstinately self-confident, including with his superiors. His words led her to think about the benefits to an individual of apologising.

Michael's words brought a smile to Zara's face. Maybe Hajj had introduced ripple-effect changes in him as well. Maybe he was on some kind of pilgrimage to being a better boss. Or maybe, Zara conceded, she was now seeing everything through a soppy spiritual lens. Whatever the explanation, Zara was still touched by Michael's words. She collected herself and continued to deliver her message, explaining the importance of seeking this forgiveness and travelling to Mecca with a clear conscience.

Before she hung up Zara said, half-joking: 'I'll pray for you.'

'I need it,' Michael laughed.

Ten weeks after deciding to go to Hajj, Zara was on a plane to Jeddah Airport in Saudi Arabia. The night before leaving, she had asked herself whether she should have started her pilgrimage duties with the *Umrah,* the smaller version of Hajj that can be performed in any month of the year. Many Muslims who feel that the expedition to Hajj is too much of a commitment in one go can begin with this experience because it requires fewer rituals, is not as physically demanding and can be performed without other pilgrims.

But there was no turning back now. The preparations for Hajj continued on the plane. A specific set of religious phrases needed to be recited, while every few hours Zara would renew her intentions for making the journey and ask Allah to open the right doors in her life.

During a stopover, she was able to spend a few moments on her own and was overcome with emotion that she would soon be on Hajj at what Muslims consider to be the divine invitation of Allah.

Once the plane landed, Zara's past anxieties about not having a *mahram* kicked in again. She had come so far and would hate to be turned back at the last minute.

As her group piled out of the plane, a vision of unity all dressed in plain, long and flowing *abayas*—a loose, robe-like garment—Zara realised that she was surrounded by women who were in the same position as her. All were drawing on the *ustatha's* many years of experience to get to their destination—and fulfil their Hajj dreams.

Clutching her documents and the *du'a* diary, it was Zara's turn to stand at the airport counter to have her paperwork checked.

Flicking through her passport, the male border control officer looked up from her identification photo: 'Zara?'

'Yes,' she smiled, trying to contain her emotions.

'Welcome, Zara.' He nodded his approval.

Zara describes Hajj as the place where she now takes herself when she is feeling down, drawing on the many happy memories and emotions of her time there. 'I have never felt at peace like I did at Hajj,' she says.

While she tries to hold on to these feelings, she has also found it hard to shake the picture of the poverty she encountered in Saudi Arabia, both among some of the locals and the pilgrims themselves. She and her fellow Australian pilgrims had been forewarned at their Hajj classes in Sydney not to give any money to beggars, of which they were told there would be many. They were informed by the more seasoned travellers that, unfortunately, most beggars were professionals and answerable to 'beggar pimps'. Even in Islam's holiest place on Earth, there would be no escaping some of life's harsh realities.

But what better time to be charitable? Zara hatched a plan to help those around her who were obviously struggling. She suggested to her group that they collect whatever small change they could spare to hand out. They would also use some of the money to buy hot meals to distribute among the poor.

Zara thought the carpark under her hotel in Mecca was a good place to start her endeavour; it resembled a highway, with swarms of buses bursting with pilgrims flying through on their way to this or that holy site.

On one of her charity nights, Zara handed out her last hot meal to a cleaner removing some rubbish. The elderly man asked her in Arabic: '*Shu, akel* [What, food]?'

'Yes, for you,' Zara confirmed, as he looked to the heavens to thank Allah for his good fortune.

But Zara was disappointed that by the time she had reached this man, her group had run out of money. Turning to one of her companions, she vowed to find him again before they left Saudi Arabia.

For her own meals in Hajj, Zara kept things simple, just as she had with her luggage. Lebanese bread filled with Nutella spread became her staple, as did the freshly-made fruit cock-tails that could be purchased from the many street stalls they encountered. She also never missed a chance to drink holy *zam-zam* water. The water's source is a well Muslims believe was miraculously generated near the *Ka'bah*. Many Muslims return from Hajj with bottles of this purifying water to hand out as gifts for family and friends.

On the last day of Hajj, Zara and her group had become accus-tomed to the local protocols of travelling by bus. As soon as their dedicated bus pulled up at any of the sites they visited, the pilgrims had to make a run for it if they were to make it onboard before it took off. Wherever they went, their bus was part of a long procession of other buses ferrying tens of thousands of pilgrims between the sites.

As she waited for their bus to the airport making its way through the throng of the hotel carpark, Zara caught a glimpse of the elderly cleaner nearby. With time against her and one eye on her bus, Zara raced up to him and placed some of the leftover local change she was still carrying into his hands.

'As I was doing this, I thought, *He was meant to get that money.*'

Muslims believe that your *rizq* (provision of wealth) comes from Allah.

While many Hajj returnees speak of the challenges that daily life presents in keeping up with the high standards that come with having completed the pilgrimage, Zara has long possessed a consciousness about her faith.

'I am not anonymous,' she declares.

Many Muslim women have this self-awareness, as the hijab marks them out as followers of their faith in the most visible of ways. This then manifests itself in how they conduct them-selves in public—swearing, littering, or displays of public affection with the opposite sex are just a few behaviours considered out of bounds. The last thing any Muslim woman wants to hear, Zara says, either from another Muslim or non-Muslim is: 'Look at what that Muslim is doing!'

To reinforce her point, Zara explains that she often finds herself drawing on a quote about the public nature of being a Muslim by American comedian Dave Chappelle, who reportedly converted to Islam in the late 1990s: 'I don't normally talk about my religion publicly because I don't want people to associate me and my flaws with this beautiful thing. And I believe it is beautiful if you learn it the right way.'

Zara, too, wants to represent the best of Islam. But she insists that she is not perfect. 'I used to react in a certain way. Now, I say, "Hang on, I'm wearing the hijab and people know I am a Muslim." I don't want to tarnish my religion, and I don't want anyone to associate my bad behaviour with something that's beautiful.'

Hajjah is the respectful title bestowed on females who have completed Hajj. It is usually associated with older women but as the number of younger Muslims travelling to Hajj is growing, so too are the number of women in Zara's generation who carry the title. Zara smiles as she divulges how her father jokingly calls her '*Hajjah al-sghiri*', or 'small *Hajjah*'. In his eyes, it is an expression not only of Zara's petite frame, but also her youth.

When she returned from Hajj, Zara decided to quit her job. She wanted a change and left on good terms. She was also determined to stay true to her Hajj commitments and continued to improve her life. And it's the little things that make a difference, she notes. One time she was a passenger in a car with a group of girlfriends who suddenly started discussing another person in an unflattering way. Zara felt uncomfortable about the position she found herself in but had the courage to explain to her friends that she wanted no part in the conversation.

'I said, "I have just come back from Hajj, and I know you don't mean anything by it, but I don't like the fact that you are talking about this person in front of me".'

Zara was careful not to put herself on a moral pedestal, but nor did she want to throw away all her hard work at Hajj on gossip. Thankfully, her girlfriends agreed.

3

Keeping the family line

Nadine is well-informed about her fertility.

She has had to be. Single and in her late thirties, she has been under pressure lately from her Lebanese-Australian family to 'just find a man and get married'. And then have a baby, because time is no longer on her side.

In the hugely successful *Bridget Jones's Diary* movie franchise, the mother of singleton Bridget explains to her daughter on FaceTime that she can have a baby on her own: 'Penny['s] . . . son sells his sperm on the internet, you don't even need a man Bridget. Some people have marvellous lives without them.'

This is not advice Nadine's Muslim mother would ever dish out, even in an age where changing societal norms and medical advances mean that women can easily have a baby without a male partner. Why? Because Islam is big on the notion of the family, which is considered the foundation of life and comprises a husband and a wife. Children must be born within a marriage. Indeed, premarital sex is considered a major sin in Islam for reasons that include the possibility of giving birth to illegitimate children.

According to research in the United Kingdom, Muslim girls are reportedly less likely to get pregnant outside of marriage than girls from all other faiths. This is because for many, being pregnant and unmarried is a major taboo, considered among the biggest of sins which brings with it cultural shame for the girl's whole family.

In countries like Australia, many young Muslims would only be educated about sex at school. While they would not be the only students whose parents do not talk to them about sex, just how taboo it remains among Muslims to have sex outside of marriage makes it an extremely loaded subject.

Nadine, who has had the opportunity to carve out a solid career as an accountant, has access to more information about getting pregnant than women have probably ever had throughout human history. She knows that for those women who are not in a position to become pregnant—due to health problems or because they are single—science can help them have a baby. IVF, egg freezing and surrogacy are a few of the options women in Nadine's position now have at their disposal.

As this list has grown, so too has the media's appetite for stories about the challenges women face in this area, especially since more women than ever graduate from university and have children later, after they have built their careers. Some of these articles are positive, others less so. In most, the message is that women need to be realistic about their poor chances of having a child later in life if they put their career ahead of trying to have a baby.

It frustrates Nadine that every time she picks up a women's magazine there is a personal element that is always missing for her in the coverage of this sensitive issue: as a Muslim, she must consider the impact of religious doctrine on these baby 'options'.

While she considers herself well-informed about the factors that could impact on her chances of having a baby (age and smoking, for example), as well as the physical challenges of leaving it too late, the biggest hurdle is that Nadine is unable to have a child on her own. Islam dictates the husband must come first, then the child. And the expectation is that she will remain a virgin until that husband is on the scene.

Nadine understands that the Quran does not comment on specific reproductive technologies, so Islamic scholars have had to form opinions over the years on modern developments based on their interpretations of the religious text. Therefore, like any of the more controversial aspects of life, the scholars don't always agree. For instance, some find it acceptable for married women to store frozen eggs for later use, while others disapprove.

Many Muslims come from ethnic backgrounds where, from a young age, the emphasis is firmly on the whole family, not the individual. Many like Nadine are brought up to consider their decisions in the context of their family and community. For some, this can be a stifling experience, though many conclude that the good outweighs the bad and decide to accept it. After all, many people with different backgrounds and beliefs do the same when navigating relationships.

At a time when society tells girls they can be anything they want to be, many Muslim women feel the added pressure of making decisions that take into account the expectations of their cultural community. Everything is then seen through the prism of the impact on this group's broader reputation. This emphasis on the family is of course not unique to Arabs or Muslims. Greek culture, for example, places the utmost importance on the family. Family members come together to support each other so that all bear the advantages of their experiences.

Despite the myriad social, economic and religious challenges many Muslim women face in some parts of the world, Nadine has been taught that mothers have a special place in Islam. Indeed, the position of the mother is elevated above the father. Special recognition is given to women who have given birth to and nursed a child, and in one *Hadith* (reports describing the sayings of the Prophet Muhammad), the Prophet said:

'Paradise is at the feet of the mother.' One interpretation of this line is that by looking after one's mother all her life, an individual will earn entry to Paradise, something to which all devout Muslims aspire. It is no surprise then that Muslims place much value on personally caring for their parents in older age or during ill health. Few Muslims would agree to put a parent in a nursing home, for instance, unless as a last medical resort.

Muslims are encouraged to have a family of their own so that an individual will always have someone to care for them. What then of those Muslims like Nadine who are single and childless? While helping to care for a sick family member, which involved taking care of their personal hygiene, it dawned on Nadine that she could not call on a daughter or son to help with the same. Turning to her married sister, she asked who would care for her if she needed it.

'I will,' her older sister responded genuinely and without hesitation, confirming the importance of family ties in Islam.

If, as an unmarried woman, Nadine were to explore her options and seek out a sperm donor for IVF, questions would be raised about the 'owner' of the sperm, as well as pressing issues such as the blurring of parental lines.

In Islam, a woman's eggs must be fertilised by her husband's sperm, otherwise she would be considered to be having someone else's child. So one thing that Islam is quite definitely against—the word *haram* (forbidden) comes up a lot in this area—is artificial insemination where the sperm donor is not the husband. In fact, it is spoken of as being akin to committing adultery. As ever, Islam's message is that lineage must at all times be kept crystal clear.

Nadine is conscious that single women in her position are increasingly deciding to freeze their eggs, so that if they meet a partner down the track, they will have access to healthier, viable eggs. When she turned to Google for stories that might illuminate Islamic principles in this area, she came across an article out of Malaysia. This particular report explained that Muslim women there are forbidden by a *fatwa* (religious edict) to freeze their eggs before marriage on a 'just-in-case' basis with the intention of using them later on.

Upon reading all this, Nadine thought: *More dead-ends.*

Twenty years ago, not long after she married, Hala became ill and spent a few years in and out of hospital. 'Having kids was not an option.'

So she was thrilled when she and her husband, Hany, tried for their first child naturally when she was 23 and conceived a son after a year.

When her son turned five, Hala agreed with Hany to have a second child. They tried for a few years without success.

Hala admits that she was at first in denial about IVF when her doctors explained to her how low were her prospects of getting pregnant without such intervention. 'They told me my best chance was IVF.'

As a practising Muslim, Hala felt slightly uneasy about the idea of using invasive technology to have a baby, even though her husband Hany's attitude was to 'go for it'.

'I really wasn't 100 per cent sure if IVF was *haram* or *halal* [permissible],' Hala recalls.

To put her mind at ease, she contacted a sheikh recommended by a trusted friend in her Lebanese-Australian community. She felt she needed to discuss the Islamic position on IVF, to check that she wasn't missing anything. As she was choosing a non-natural way to have a child, she thought Islam would surely have a position on it. What Hala was hoping for was a *fatwa* from the sheikh that she was on the right path and not doing anything that went against her religion.

When Hala phoned the sheikh, she had to leave a message. The next day, when she was a passenger in her sister-in-law's car, the sheikh returned her call. She knew as soon as she took the call that talking to him in this situation wasn't ideal but, now that she had him on the line, she didn't want to miss her chance.

Hala went through her story with the sheikh. She calmly explained her past medical problems, that she had her first child naturally and how her doctors had recently informed her that her best chance of having another baby was through IVF.

But she was left shaken by the sheikh's response.

'He said that using IVF was *haram*. I don't think I heard the rest of the conversation.'

Her sister-in-law, behind the wheel, had grown anxious when she detected Hala's tone becoming more and more despondent. 'What happened? What did he say?' she asked breathlessly when the call concluded.

A stunned Hala managed to tell her sister-in-law that the sheikh did not support her use of IVF.

'That can't be right,' her sister-in-law said repeatedly while trying to focus on the traffic.

Hala is slightly embarrassed as she tells the story of how she first met Hany as a teenager. She was talking with her best friend, Zena, over a two-way CB radio. The girls had somehow managed to convince their very conservative fathers to buy them car batteries to power the radios. It was in the days before mobile phones became the norm, Hala explains.

One Saturday afternoon, when boredom was starting to get the better of her, Hala got on the radio with Zena, who went to the same high school and lived only a few suburbs away. As the girls caught up, Hany happened to be listening in with an acquaintance of Hala's family, who had recognised her 'call name', Poppy. After the boys playfully interrupted the conversation, Hala and Hany got talking. Everyone on the radio was conscious of the lack of privacy, as anyone, anywhere and at any time could listen in on their talk simply by turning the dial to their channel. Though all of the participants accepted that this was one of the downsides of using the radio, it never stopped them from playing with it.

'It was like an open chatroom,' Hala reminisces, stressing that she and her friends were careful to stick to mundane questions such as, 'How are you? What are you doing? Who's around?'

Hala and Hany got along so well that they became engaged when she was nineteen and married a year later. While they can boast that they came together after first communicating on the public airwaves, their IVF journey was a much more private affair—and continues to be.

The only other people who knew that Hala wanted to try IVF were her parents and also Hany's, with whom she had developed a good relationship. She had intentionally kept the information tight to avoid the stigma attached to this type of medical intervention in her community at the time.

When Hala first explained to her parents-in-law what the sheikh had told her, they were as surprised as she had been—and unconvinced that it was a sound religious ruling.

Twenty or so years ago, when she married Hany, there had been a common fear among Muslim women in her community, even in Australia, that if they could not give their husbands a child, divorce or a second wife as part of an Islamic marriage (that is, one not registered with the government) were inevitable. The thinking was that any man was entitled to seek out another wife so he could have a family of his own.

Then a decade ago, when IVF was being accessed more widely, there was still a prejudice expressed within Hala's community that women who could not have a child naturally were somehow damaged.

'If she can't get pregnant, there's something wrong with her,' was the hurtful line trotted out, Hala recalls. At that time, there was not the amount of positive information about IVF there is now, nor the broad level of acceptance.

Refusing to accept that Hala and Hany could not grow their family, her father-in-law decided to take matters into his own hands. He had great faith in the scholarly experience of a sheikh from one of the bigger mosques in Sydney and set up an appointment for himself, on his daughter-in-law's behalf, to seek guidance from this man.

While Hala had been encouraged to seek another opinion herself, Islam discourages '*fatwa* shopping', where individuals attempt to get the answer they want to hear. As a *fatwa* is an Islamic legal opinion, the aim is that they should be standardised so that individuals are not tempted to ask different sheikhs for advice until they like what they are told. In their daily lives, Muslims are advised to seek out regular advice from the same trusted and qualified religious leader, not to jump from one to the next.

Hala had been too upset by the advice she had initially received to tell anyone about her father-in-law's appointment: 'I didn't want to set myself up again for disappointment. When I was first told IVF is *haram*, I was quite devastated and didn't want the sheikh to elaborate because I had put my faith in him and my hopes were no longer high. I thought, *It's in God's hands, that is what God has written for me, not to have a second child.*'

But she need not have worried this time around. The advice her father-in-law received from the sheikh was that if she was not using a donor—if it was her own eggs and her husband's sperm—then it was *halal* for her to pursue IVF.

'Go ahead and do it,' her father-in-law told her confidently after his meeting.

When she was 33, Hala gave birth to a daughter through IVF. At the time, she also decided to freeze some embryos for potential later use. As part of the IVF process for her daughter, as many of her eggs as possible were fertilised. The best one was then implanted, while the rest were frozen for up to ten years. This was the total IVF package for which Hala had paid.

Recently, Hala and Hany thought they would try for a third child. One of the leftover embryos—the one considered to be the most viable—was implanted into Hala. But it did not take and, after everything she and Hany had been through to have children over the years, as well as the financial cost of rejoining the IVF program and her age, they decided not to continue.

'If it was going to happen, it was going to happen when the defrosted embryo was implanted,' Hala believes.

She is convinced that if the sheikh who was more informed about this area of Islamic jurisprudence had not given her the green light, she would not have pursued IVF for fear that she would be going against God. Her fears centred on tempting fate and having an unhealthy child.

All these years later, there is much more information in the public domain about the success rates of IVF. 'Now in the community it's more accepted than it was back then,' Hala confirms.

Nonetheless, she chooses not to make it generally known that her daughter was born through IVF due to continuing cultural misconceptions. In particular, she doesn't want uninformed people thinking there is something wrong with her daughter.

Despite her own successful experience, Hala herself draws the line at Muslim couples using someone else's eggs or sperm to have a child.

'At the end of the day,' she says quite vehemently, 'you are going to have a child from someone else. Don't even bother asking a sheikh about doing such a thing—it's not an option.'

One of the continuing concerns about donor eggs and sperm in Islam is that an IVF child may grow up to inadvertently marry their sibling. When challenged that the chances of this happening in the modern era are miniscule, Hala's opposition remains unwavering. 'But it could happen. If I did not have my eggs and my husband's sperm, then that would have been the end of the line for me. That's the way Allah wants it.'

Not every woman who wants a child can have one.

This harsh reality is something with which Sonia has had to contend.

At eighteen, she became engaged to Saleh, who is two years older and shares her Afghan-Australian background. Explaining why she formalised their relationship at such a young age, she says, 'In my culture, I couldn't move in with him until we got married.'

Years earlier, her path to Australia with her family had taken her from Afghanistan at the age of five to India for seven years. At twelve, they moved to Australia as refugees. Establishing her new life here, Sonia admits that she became less interested than she already had been in her Sunni/Islamic roots. But her husband was even less so. This has led to arguments, for example, about her decision to fast during Ramadan; once, Saleh even threatened to divorce her over the issue. Despite her limited observance of Islamic practices, Sonia held her ground, telling him he could not stop her from undertaking the fast.

Sonia has taken note of other religious expectations, too. When she joined her parents on a trip to their home city of Kabul five years ago to visit relatives, Sonia says she had to wear a hijab as she moved around the conservative city. Before travelling overseas, she had openly expressed concern to her family about the potential for violence in Afghanistan, the kind that she had often seen on the news. She even asked, 'What if someone chops my head off?' Her family had dismissed her concerns. And contrary to common perceptions, Sonia found that Kabul was not just a place of war. Not only was she able to get around easily, she wore the hijab very loosely in public with much of her hair exposed, without experiencing harassment from any quarters. Further, despite decades of conflict, Sonia was pleasantly surprised to find a very modern side to Kabul, one that included shopping centres and quality restaurants.

When Sonia and Saleh married four years after they became engaged, Sonia was studying at university and agreed with Saleh that they weren't ready yet for a baby. Her husband was adamant that he was too young for such a commitment, so after Sonia unexpectedly became pregnant, they both decided not to go through with it.

This is a taboo subject in Muslim circles, as abortion—especially for social reasons—is considered by many as strictly forbidden. Based on anecdotal evidence, however, the practice is on the rise among Muslims in Australia, a development that is rarely discussed openly.

Sonia concedes that she did not think about the matter from a religious perspective at all. She just did what she needed to do at the time: 'Saleh wasn't ready to have kids, and I didn't want to either.' She kept their decision a secret, although Saleh's parents later found out after one of their many major arguments over his reticence to start a family.

Two years after the abortion, Sonia, then in her mid twenties, had completed her studies and was ready to become a mother. 'But my husband still wasn't ready.'

Their different views about having a baby had become a source of conflict between Sonia and Saleh. It wasn't until many years into their marriage that Sonia was able to finally convince him to try for a child. In the meantime, she had grown exasperated with his lack of interest in starting a family.

Anxious to get pregnant, Sonia now found she was unable to do so naturally. As her desperation grew, she turned to religion on her mother's advice, even though she admits she is barely observant.

'I visited a sheikh with my mum and told him my problems, that I had not been able to have a baby,' Sonia recalls.

'He read passages to me from the Quran and told me that someone had given me the evil eye. He then took out a small piece of paper, wrote some lines on it and said to put it in my husband's teapot. That would help us break the curse and I would have a baby.'

As they left, she handed the sheikh the $100 he requested for his spiritual guidance. Some cultures that practise Islam believe receiving the evil eye leads to misfortune. But Sonia admits that even her mother, who is more religious than she, thought the sheikh's advice was more akin to magic than Islam and questioned his bona fides.

'I did it just once: I put the paper in the teapot, and then threw the paper away,' Sonia says, shaking her head. 'I realised soon after that having a child is up to God.'

Confused more than ever, but prepared to grab at anything that might help her have a baby, Sonia visited a private medical clinic where she was advised by a doctor that, if she had a small operation, she would get pregnant within three to six months. His services were pricier than the sheikhs'—$4000, a sum which the doctor emphasised he wanted in cash. The procedure would involve day surgery and Sonia would need to take a day off work.

Saleh knew Sonia had consulted a doctor, and was sceptical when she told him about the procedure. He told her that no proper doctor could make such a claim. Sonia was dejected that Saleh rejected the idea as soon as he heard it, and did not dare to mention the cost of the operation as she feared it would only make matters worse.

'The way the doctor spoke to me, he convinced me it would happen within six months,' Sonia says.

Despite her husband's doubts, she was undeterred.

When Sonia returned home from the clinic following the procedure, she was tired and in a little pain. She went to bed early that night, telling Saleh she was getting her period and had cramps. He did not suspect a thing.

More than six months passed and nothing changed for Sonia. Her mother urged her to formally complain about the doctor, but Sonia did not have the emotional energy to do so, especially since Saleh was unaware of what she had done. She knew he would also be upset that she had borrowed some of the money for the procedure from her mother and sister, which she was slowly paying back.

Sonia has had to move on and is now convinced that IVF might help. Once again, though, she has hit a brick wall with Saleh, who says he wants her to have a child naturally—he fears their child could have medical problems if they use IVF. Sonia does not share his concerns, which could be allayed by medical professionals if only he were open-minded.

Just as Saleh is adamant in his opposition to IVF, so too is Sonia strong in her views that she does not want to foster a child. She dreams of being pregnant and having her own baby. So deep is this urge—even seeing photos of her friends with their young children on Facebook has become painful—that she is dismissive of the idea of caring for a child to whom she has not given birth.

Whether her attitude will soften has yet to be seen. But the disappointments of the past few years have left Sonia questioning her relationship with Saleh. She is so determined to have a child that she has even contemplated leaving him and trying for one with someone else. Perhaps it could work with another person, she has wondered. In her cultural circles, especially overseas, it is usually the man who would take such a drastic stance, while the woman is expected to suffer in silence and spend her life childless or with a man who has taken a second wife to have children.

On one occasion, unhappy for the umpteenth time with his casual attitude about a baby, Sonia left Saleh. She soon felt terrible and returned home.

Like this episode, Sonia's feelings about her inability so far to have a baby are constantly shifting and changing. For now, she is trying to accept her life, including the idea that she might not be a mother.

'If a child is meant for me, it will happen,' she says stoically, oblivious to the spiritual undertones of her words.

4

Time willing

Ayesha, her sister Amal, and her two brothers—all four grown-up and in their thirties and forties—are currently engaged in a robust conversation about inheritance.

Their parents are getting older; the family home in Sydney, which was purchased more than three decades ago, has become a very valuable asset. Indeed, when they first migrated to Australia from Lebanon, Ayesha's parents could never have imagined that their children's debate would play out against a backdrop where the average price of a suburban home is pushing the million-dollar mark.

One of her brothers is especially unmoved by Ayesha's argument that she and her sister should receive an equal share of the estate because they have contributed as much to their parents' wealth as the brothers have over the years, be it through paying bills for living expenses, funding overseas holidays or contributing to gifts. This is not to mention the time spent on unpaid care for their parents.

This brother takes seriously the religious position that he has financial responsibilities towards his wife and parents that his sisters will never have. The second brother is younger and doesn't argue against the idea that his two sisters should receive the same share as him. He doesn't know that much about Sharia; he has always been less traditional and encouraged his sisters to be independent and to fulfil their dreams.

When they are alone together after any family discussion about this, Amal angrily calls out her brothers to Ayesha: 'They shouldn't get more, and they should be the ones suggesting to our parents—while they are still with us—that we all get the same. Why should we have to do the dirty work by asking about it?'

Time will tell how this debate plays out.

'I get more than you because I'm a boy!' Ayesha recalls her older brother teasing her when they played together as children.

It was a sharp barb, even though she knew her brother was stirring her, but it was also a line that he had parroted ever since his mother had told him as a young boy that he was different to his sisters. From a young age, many Muslim boys in Australia are raised to expect that, under Sharia, they will inherit a bigger slice of the family's wealth than their sisters.

Ayesha's brother was on the money: according to Sharia, a brother is entitled to double the share of a sister. This religious argument is rooted in the idea that, in the Islamic world, men are expected to use their inheritance to support the family unit, including their wives, elderly parents and unmarried sisters. Women have no such religious obligations and can spend their money on themselves.

While under Islamic law, all of a woman's income is considered discretionary and solely her own, in today's reality the income would likely contribute to household budgets in the same way as that of a man. However, the woman's contribution is considered an act of generosity—and not one that impacts on her formal share of inheritance. Why? Because if a woman is improving relationships by helping her family financially when she is not religiously obligated to, then such deeds will be recognised by Allah and she will be rewarded for her endeavours in the afterlife.

The application of the inheritance laws is compulsory in Islamic countries, because the way in which Muslims inherit is set down in the Quran, and women who are left without financial support by their obligated male family member(s) can take up the matter in court. Muslims in secular countries follow these practices voluntarily, however, in Australian

Muslim communities at least, exactly how the inheritance rules should apply is becoming a growing source of debate and potential legal conflict.

As Islam defines the rights and responsibilities of every family member, only those with a blood relationship to the deceased and who are born as part of an Islamic marriage can inherit, which excludes step-children and fostered or illegitimate children as their lineage is not traced back to the father. There is a provision (especially among Sunnis) that one can bequeath up to a third of one's assets to non-heirs. This discretion with one's estate does not extend to natural heirs as they are already formally recognised.

It may be hard to fathom, but inheritance laws in Islam are not based on emotion or sentiment. Muslims see themselves as trustees on Earth of any assets they come into courtesy of Allah, and Allah asks a Muslim to dispose of it in certain ways both during one's life and after death. Muslims believe that, when they die, their estate must meet four obligations: funeral and burial expenses must be paid; all personal debts must be met; the value of the estate must be determined; and the distribution of the remaining estate to relatives must be in accordance with Sharia. Certain relatives—any living spouse, parents, sons and daughters—are always entitled to a share under Islam. Muslims can also be involved with *waqf*, a charitable endowment which often involves donating or dedicating land for religious purposes.

Viewed on its own, the rule that a son's share must be twice that of a daughter is often perceived as unfair, even among Muslims. Considered against the backdrop of Islamic law as a whole, however, the religion sets out many financial responsibilities for men that are not expected of women, and the inheritance laws are built into these responsibilities. In addition, women are entitled to a *mahr* (dowry) from a husband upon marriage, and this is described by some scholars as an 'advance of inheritance rights from her husband's estate'.

Ayesha was born and raised in Australia, where specific inheritance practises—including any share entitlements for the children of the deceased—are not enshrined by law. She therefore knows that she could ultimately legally challenge any decision that gives her brothers a bigger portion than her or her sister. That is one of the good things about living in Australia, she tells herself. However, she is conflicted about ever acting on this, as she is acutely aware that such a move would violate her parents' deeply-held religious wishes on the matter. Even if she felt cheated financially, it would be hard for Ayesha not to respect their position since they truly believe that if they thumb their nose at this Islamic rule they will be punished in the afterlife for breaking Sharia.

Ayesha recalls the time her father reiterated his view at a family meeting called ahead of a long-planned trip back to his native Lebanon with her mother: If anything happened to them while they were overseas, he wanted Sharia to be observed in the division of their assets in Australia. No one spoke out against his position; out of respect, Ayesha and Amal had held back their thoughts.

If a Muslim is confused about what they are entitled to under Sharia inheritance laws, they need look no further than one of the online Islamic calculators that provide answers on inheritance for every type of relationship.

Ayesha was very curious about what would happen in various scenarios and clicked on one of the calculators to read the advice it provided. She could scroll through a total of 134 'test cases' if she so pleased.

According to the calculator, where the heirs to a Sydney home worth $1 million that had no debts against it are two sons and two daughters, the brothers would stand to gain $333,333 each while the sisters would be allocated $166,666 each.

Looking at the hard numbers in this way, the difference was stark. It was also a reality check and got Ayesha thinking about her own mortality. She has never married and has no children. Because she lives at home with her parents, she has been able to save enough money for a deposit on an investment property and over the years has made inroads into paying down her mortgage due to a good salary.

Many thoughts started swirling in her head. What if her personal circumstances didn't change and she died after her parents? She discovered that the Islamic inheritance rules decree that her brothers would inherit all of her property, a picture that leaves Ayesha very uncomfortable, as she wants to leave Amal an equal share. While she loves her brothers and Amal equally, she is especially close to Amal. Why should Amal be left with less than her brothers in this situation? Ayesha realised that she would have to give serious thought to how her will dealt with this matter, and she would have to dig deep into her conscience to decide if she would disregard Sharia on inheritance when it came to her own life.

Are there any situations where it's the reverse, and parents inherit from their children? Ayesha wondered. She turned to the calculator again and got her answer: Where a woman dies, for example, and there are no children and only her husband and parents are left behind, then the husband receives only half, while her father receives one-third and her mother one-sixth.

One Turkish-Australian woman took a more forceful approach to inheritance than Ayesha and Amal are likely to contemplate. Reportedly, she challenged her brothers in a Canberra court for an equal share of her mother's, Mariem Omari's, estate, arguing that she should get the same amount regardless of gender. As it stood under Islamic rules of inheritance, her three brothers would inherit one full share for every half-share allocated to her and her four sisters.

The daughter argued that the will was invalid, as her mother had been suffering dementia and hadn't been of sound mind when she signed the document in the presence of her sons. The sons argued that, as a devout Muslim who prayed, fasted and performed a pilgrimage to Mecca, their mother would have ensured her will followed Islamic principles.

As the court proceedings unfolded, the legal argument focused principally on whether Mariem had had sufficient mental capacity to make a will; the brothers' arguments that the will should be divided along Islamic law lines became legally irrelevant. In the end, the court decided that Mariem had died intestate. Still, this case provided an important example of how a Muslim woman in Australia was prepared to challenge inheritance based on Sharia. As the Muslim population in Australia ages, Ayesha considers this case a sign of things to come.

For one Muslim couple, the application of the inheritance rules has led to more questions than answers. Hana and her husband Tarek, both the children of migrants from Lebanon, have done well for themselves, with Hana in many ways the backbone of her family's early financial success. Her decision to open a small business became a turning point for the family.

With both Hana and Tarek now regularly travelling overseas to stock up on products for their store, Hana felt the need to discuss with Tarek whether they should draw up a will and if they needed to consider any religious rules. In particular, she was focused on what would happen to their estate if they were both killed in an accident.

When she first broached the subject with Tarek, he was dismissive. Hana put this down to how most people—regardless of their background—react to this sensitive topic. But she persisted and, as she did so, she began to develop an understanding of what Tarek wanted. And for the first time she realised that his position was not necessarily the same as hers.

Tarek was keen for his older sister to step in if anything happened to them; he trusted her to care for their three children (a daughter and two sons). For Hana, it didn't sit right that Tarek's sister would have the biggest say in her children's future while her family would be relegated to the sidelines. She had always thought that her own sister and brother would also be involved if anything ever were to happen to her, and have a role to play in guiding and supporting her children to make the best decisions for their future.

Hana knew that her own brother stood to gain more than her and her sister on the death of their parents, who had purchased two Sydney properties. Her family had already witnessed how messy inheritance could become: after Hana's grandparents died, her father, uncles and aunts had to work hard to resolve their differences about how to divide their property. The inheritance took a long time to sort out, as the matter was complicated by the fact that some adult children had lived with the elderly couple, while others resided overseas. Eventually, the grandparents' home was sold and the money split among the children according to Sharia.

Hana is keen for her children to avoid the same problems. For now, however, she is considering approaching a solicitor— so that she and Tarek can tidy up any loose ends and agree on the best way forward—and intends to educate herself further on the Islamic inheritance rules. She accepts the idea they exist for a reason. 'These things are complex and one's family situation plays a big role. If the family is united and there is respect, things should work out.'

Importantly, her daughter is now at an age where she is mature enough to look after her two younger brothers if anything should happen to their parents.

Even if Hana has faith that the issue would sort itself out in a positive way for her children, Ayesha is mindful that any disputes would be about the share that women inherit, not the notion of inheritance itself. This has also been a topic of debate that continues today among Muslim scholars.

Ayesha notes that over the years, when she has been critical of the brother–sister inheritance divide, she had been informed that assets could be passed on to children as a gift during the life of a parent without consideration to gender. And in Arab culture, daughters traditionally inherit their mother's gold jewellery, an important component of the *mahr*. Such assets can amount to substantial collections. While efforts can be made to even the ledger between sons and daughters in advance of death, Ayesha is not convinced about this method as a form of equalisation. She can't help but wonder: 'Human nature being what it is, how many people really think about giving away their wealth during their lifetime?'

5

Broken engagement

One Saturday afternoon, Jihan and Mazen gathered together their family and friends. Arabic music played softly in the background while more than fifty guests took their seats in the garden of Jihan's family home, alongside long buffets of Lebanese finger food, sweets and coffee.

As Jihan and Mazen, accompanied by their fathers, made their way to a decorated couch at one end of the gathering the crowd clapped their approval.

The music was switched off to allow for the religious part of the engagement ceremony to take place. Led by a sheikh, the couple publicly agreed to adhere to certain conditions as husband and wife. Jihan promised to respect and care for Mazen; he reciprocated. Among other things, he would also pay for her to join him on a pilgrimage to Mecca within the first five years of their marriage.

In Australia, wedding ceremonies generally coincide with the completion of official paperwork under civil law. In the eyes of Islam, however, a couple can sign an Islamic marriage contract, as Jihan and Mazen did at their engagement party, but wait to live together following a formal wedding ceremony, which might take place months or even years later. The signing of the civil certificate can follow the Islamic marriage, though some couples choose only to marry religiously.

While Jihan and Mazen were married according to Islam and entitled to enjoy the various rights and responsibilities that come with this, their Lebanese cultural background required that their marriage be ultimately completed as part of a public celebration marked as their wedding day. Jihan and Mazen planned to hold their wedding in about a year's time, as this would give them some breathing space to save their money.

The couple had met through one of Mazen's aunts, who lived on the same street as Jihan's family and had become a regular visitor to their home. The aunt, who had gotten to know Jihan quite well, suggested to the young woman one day over lunch that she might like Mazen and that they should meet.

Jihan, who had recently turned 23, was open to the idea of a relationship; Mazen, who was a year older than her, had been back in Australia for a few years. He was born here, but grew up in Lebanon with his parents and returned with them after his father struggled to earn a living overseas.

The two had only known each other for a few months before Jihan announced to her parents that Mazen wanted to ask them for her hand in marriage. This was the first time her parents had heard about this developing relationship. They expected that, until it had been formalised at the engagement ceremony, Jihan would do the right thing religiously and only be in Mazen's company with a family member present. In the meantime, one of Jihan's younger sisters would act as their chaperone, joining Jihan and Mazen on any trips they made together outside her home. Despite mixing with the opposite sex in their everyday lives, this was to protect them from gossip, as their families were conservative and only wanted them to spend time alone together after they had signed their Islamic marriage contract at their engagement.

Even with such a document signed, though, Jihan and Mazen found that their parents still preferred they did not sit alone. The two were soon craving much greater freedom. It had become increasingly difficult to work around Jihan's younger sister's schedule every time they wanted to go out. They were both exhausted and at times embarrassed by the organisation all this required, which they were only doing out of respect for their parents.

Just a few months after the engagement party, Jihan became suspicious of Mazen's behaviour. He had been making excuses about why he could not spend time with her, often complaining that he was too tired to see her after work. One night, she visited Mazen's work unannounced.

She soon found herself trailing Mazen's car. At a set of traffic lights on a busy road, she pulled up alongside him and saw that there was a woman in the passenger's seat. Mazen turned his head and suddenly recognised Jihan—he was visibly shocked as Jihan began gesturing for Mazen to call her.

Mazen finally contacted her a few hours later—he wanted to give her time to calm down, he said—and attempted to explain that the woman was simply a colleague who needed a lift home after finishing late. But seeing the woman in the car with Mazen confirmed to Jihan that she hadn't been imagining things: Mazen had withdrawn from her, and she knew there was much more to it than he was suggesting.

The next morning, she worked up the courage to tell her father, Sam, what had happened. She had worried all night about what to do; her mobile phone had been going off every hour as Mazen tried to contact her again, to talk her out of breaking things off.

The thing Sam valued the most in life after his family was going to work so that he could make enough money to look after them. Jihan had gotten to know Mazen without much involvement from her family, but now that she was in trouble, she had no one else to turn to. As she was technically married under Islam, it would not be easy to end things with Mazen. Her sheikh would need to adjudicate on the divorce.

Jihan was relieved at how quickly her father took control of the situation. Despite protests from Mazen's father for his son and Jihan to try to work things out, Sam was adamant that the two families should visit the sheikh who had presided over the engagement to discuss the terms of a divorce as soon as possible.

Jihan knew the sheikh well—he was related to her father and had often been around when she was growing up. The sheikh had a reputation in the community for fairness and, despite his closeness to Jihan's family, Mazen's father trusted him to be independent.

However, Jihan herself did not expect any favours. She remembered that, when she was little, the sheikh had been fond of commenting on what was or was not appropriate for a girl. This had frustrated her, because each time it meant that her parents would become a little stricter with her and her sisters. The list of things girls could not do—like riding a bicycle—was a long one.

Jihan felt considerable anxiety on her way to meeting the sheikh. She was taken aback by his first request: he wanted each of them to tell him the pros and cons of their relationship. This was not some chat that she was having with a girlfriend, Jihan thought. She took a deep breath and tried to convince herself that it was the sheikh's way of seeing things from all perspectives.

Mazen went first. The thing he liked the least about Jihan, he said, was her constant questioning of his whereabouts. Jihan rolled her eyes and inhaled loudly. *Does Mazen not realise the irony of what he's saying?* she wondered. She wanted to scream that he had amply demonstrated he could not be trusted.

Jihan's father sensed her frustration and shot her a glance that made her feel uncomfortable. It was a look she had known since childhood; now, even as an adult, she knew exactly what it meant—she needed to mind her behaviour.

But her unease was alleviated by the sheikh's response to Mazen's complaint: a woman should know where her fiancée is going and what he is doing, the sheikh said. He always told his wife where he was.

'If the sheikh can do it . . .' Jihan whispered incredulously under her breath.

Mazen had maintained from the start that he had not been doing anything wrong when Jihan followed him that night. He had only offered to drive a colleague home. At first, he had strongly resisted the idea of ending things with Jihan, but a few minutes into the meeting, it was starting to dawn on him that perhaps he and Jihan weren't good together and he started to change his tone.

That's when the sheikh got serious, too. He pulled out a pocket-sized Quran, the cover elegantly decorated in Arabic calligraphy, and asked Mazen to prove himself by holding it in both hands and swearing an oath that he was telling the truth about driving the woman home.

From a young age, many Muslims learn that if they tell a lie while touching the holy book, they are sentencing themselves to a stint in hell. The Quranic oath is taken so seriously that even those who are not overly religious would think twice about swearing it falsely. Some strict Muslims disagree altogether with using this hand-on-Quran tactic, arguing it is not a mature approach to solving serious problems.

Nevertheless, it came as no surprise to Jihan that Mazen refused to take the oath. He argued that his word should be enough. But his refusal came with consequences.

The sheikh ruled in Jihan's favour. This was an important ruling, as it meant that Jihan was the wronged party in the relationship, a decision that would have implications for her financial rights under the Islamic marriage contract, especially since Mazen was now agreeing that they should no longer be together.

The conversation turned now to the contract's *mahr* clause. The sheikh pointed out that, since Mazen was at fault and also wanted to end the relationship, under that contract he owed Jihan $25,000 for violating it. Though there are conflicting religious and cultural positions on this, the sheikh's approach

was one generally adopted by Sunni Muslims in such circumstances. At the mention of money, Mazen's father sprung to
his son's defence, pleading with the sheikh to reconsider. He
argued that, because the couple had not consummated their
relationship, Jihan had kept her sexual purity—a big plus in his
mind, since it would make it easier for her to move on. His son
could also not afford to pay such a large sum.

Jihan was angered by this argument: why did her rights,
as set out in the Islamic marriage contract, have to be rene-
gotiated? Why did Mazen and his family agree to the terms
in the first place if they weren't going to honour them? Why
shouldn't Mazen have to pay for treating her badly?

When she had signed the papers at the ceremony, Jihan
had never thought that she would be in this position. Now,
she was determined to get everything to which she was religiously entitled. So she turned to Mazen's father and asked:
'Why did you write that amount and sign on it if you weren't
going to take it seriously?'

Her father-in-law had nominated—in fact, insisted—on the
$25,000 because it was the same amount that he had requested
for his own daughter upon her marriage. It was his way of
showing that he thought of Jihan as a daughter. With his son
now in trouble, though, it was obvious to Jihan whose side he
was on—it had nothing to do with what was right and everything to do with money.

In many Middle Eastern communities, one part of the *mahr* is provided to a woman in the lead-up to her wedding, to be spent on jewellery and preparations for a home. The remaining amount—agreed on in advance by both parties in the Islamic marriage contract—can come into play in the event that things turn sour. It is a recognition that a woman in these circumstances no longer has a man to rely on for her basic financial support, a responsibility that falls on all men under Islam. However, a sheikh could also decide that a man is the innocent party and his wife has to repay the dowry to formally end a relationship.

If there is one area where Islamic law has arguably been more liberal than Western society, it is in the area of divorce. Divorce in Islam is allowed and can be initiated by either the husband or wife. However, that Islam permits divorce should not be interpreted as Islam being soft on divorce. Quite the contrary, as the dissolution of a marriage is usually strongly resisted, even condemned. Religious leaders are loath to divorce couples, and specific, compelling reasons are usually required. Indeed, in many Muslim communities, community elders would be called on to attempt to reconcile the couple before any final decisions are taken.

Despite the clearly-defined Islamic position on women's rights regarding divorce, how Muslim women are treated in a modern divorce can be a problem, as patriarchal cultural attitudes continue to disadvantage many, regardless of whether they live in a Muslim or non-Muslim country.

In Jihan's case, Mazen had promised a $25,000 dowry upfront
to cover expenses, including a diamond ring, and another
$25,000 that would be paid if the relationship ended and he
was to blame.

Jihan worked at an employment agency and was paid
reasonably well. She also knew that her family would always
help her out with money if she needed it. At this moment,
though, as she sat in the sheikh's office, the notion that she had
the ability to support herself financially was beside the point.

'Am I worth nothing?' she began to cry, shaking her head in
disbelief at the stance taken by her father-in-law.

Jihan's father shot her another displeased look. He was
worried about how emotional his daughter was becoming
and it was important to him that she maintain a certain level
of respect towards Mazen's family, especially in the presence of
the sheikh.

They had been meeting with the sheikh for some two
hours without a break and Jihan was starting to feel defeated.
She turned to Mazen's father and in a firm voice explained
that she no longer wanted his family's money, but not before
adding that she would never forgive his son for not paying her
what had been promised and was within her rights.

Mazen's father was mortified by her threat. He knew exactly
what it meant: as a Muslim, owing this money would be a
millstone around his son's neck for the rest of his life—and in

the afterlife, too. In Islam, a debt is not forgiven until it is paid or the person owed the money forgives it.

The sheikh now stepped in: 'Would you pay $17,000?' he asked Mazen's father.

Such bartering angered Jihan all over again. 'Why are you negotiating the figure down?' she asked the sheikh, trying to sound as polite as she could, under the circumstances.

But she was too late. Mazen's father saw an opening: 'I will pay $10,000.'

The sheikh turned to Jihan and in a reassuring voice explained that she needed to accept that, if Mazen could not pay the original agreed sum, then it was better to take what she could get. When making a decision about such a clause in a marriage contract, it was his role to also take into account an individual's personal circumstances, including their capacity to pay.

Jihan persisted with the sheikh, making it personal: 'Would you do the same if it were your daughter?'

'Yes, I would,' he replied without hesitation. He looked Jihan in the eye and continued: 'God said that, if you can be the better person, then be the better person.'

'And get less money,' Jihan whispered under her breath.

But the sheikh had spoken, and Jihan was conscious that her father did not want to leave without a resolution. Knowing what she knew about Mazen's thin finances, she resigned herself to the fact that it was the best deal that she was going to get. Besides, she was tired, weighed down by all her emotions.

Sensing that Jihan was waning, and keen to bring matters to a close, the sheikh turned to Mazen and warned him: 'If you were in Saudi Arabia, you would have gotten a hundred lashes for what you did.'

Jihan waited to hear Mazen say something meaningful, to express regret for his actions and accept his wrongdoing. Instead, he sat stony-faced, unmoved even by the mention of a lashing.

Jihan tried hard not to show it, but she was devastated by how things had turned out. She felt that not only had Mazen betrayed her, he had dodged his responsibilities as well. She would be the one left with a stain on her reputation, as men in her community faced less prejudice than women when they moved on from relationships. It dawned on her that she was a divorced woman before she had even really been married.

In the months that followed, Jihan leaned heavily on her family and friends for support. She worked hard to get another qualification to improve her prospects at work. She was also pleasantly surprised by how quickly she was able to meet other Muslim men, none of whom judged her—at least not to her face—about her failed relationship.

Still, it took a while for her to connect with someone who was able to make her feel like they had a future together.

Several years passed. One day while she was at work, Jihan received an unexpected phone call from her father telling her that the sheikh wanted them to visit that night. Since the sheikh was still a regular visitor to her family's home, she could not easily make excuses to turn him down. Besides, she was a justice of the peace and the sheikh often required her signature; she assumed this was the reason he wanted to see her and she took her civic responsibilities very seriously.

As agreed, Jihan met her father at the sheikh's house that night. She had become so comfortable in the sheikh's presence since her Islamic divorce that she almost immediately asked him if he had a document he wanted her to look at.

'I have something better,' he said, passing an envelope to her.

'Did you win the Lotto and feel sorry for me?' Jihan joked as she played with the bulky package, which she guessed contained some cash.

'It's from Mazen—his father gave me the money,' the sheikh replied.

Jihan had convinced herself a long time ago that she would never see the money owed to her. Despite agreeing to the lesser sum, Mazen's family had not wanted a deadline to be set for payment and had asked for some time for it to be saved. Jihan had assumed that this was code for non-payment and eventually moved on without relying on it.

Now her head was swirling with questions. The sheikh's tone—which had softened towards her over the intervening years—had become serious again. He asked her to count the money he had handed to her, $100 note by $100 note, and to do so in front of a witness—an elderly female relative of his who was also well-known to Jihan's family. This would help to avoid a dispute down the track from any of the parties about the exact sum of money that had been delivered to the sheikh.

The old woman had a reputation for being discreet and conservative; she was the type of person who no doubt would have been sensible with the money if she had been in Jihan's shoes. She had also come prepared. To assist with the task ahead, she handed Jihan a bunch of elastic bands with which to wrap the loose notes.

Perhaps sensing some hesitation on Jihan's part, she leaned in and calmly suggested: 'Give a small amount to charity and spend the rest on heels.'

6

Separate quarters

When Mona's parents, Bilal and Layla, had adult friends over, it was not like when she visited her friends and everyone sat in the same living room.

While the free-flowing spaces of open-plan living are all the rage on home-renovation television shows, the experience was more closed in the suburban Sydney home of Mona's parents, where she grew up.

When men visited her father, they knew not to knock on the front door but to walk down the side of the house to a back entry. There, they were met by Bilal or one of Mona's brothers and led to a living room. The men could never cross paths with Mona's mother or her sisters, who all lived in the same house. Even when the women prepared drinks and snacks in the kitchen for these guests, a male family member would be responsible for taking them away and serving the men.

Female visitors would come through the front entrance—often parting ways with their husbands at the front gate. Once inside, they would set themselves up in a second living room down the hallway from the men; here, they too could never cross paths with Mona's father or any other males in the house.

In some Middle Eastern countries, homes are designed with one entrance for men and another for women, so that non-related males do not enter 'female zones'. It is said that they are set out in this way to ensure a family's honour is protected. In an Australian setting, Mona's parents, who come from an Iraqi Shia background, are practicing the same gender segregation in their home.

Before she married, Mona's home life was underpinned by religious rules that often blurred with cultural mores heavily shaped by the social gatherings that had unfolded inside her parents' childhood homes in their native Iraq. When people came together there, they congregated in groups divided along gender lines. It was how things were done, and are mostly still done. There was nothing particularly offensive or overtly religious about this segregation, Mona believed—it was not dissimilar to what one might see at a typical Sunday barbecue in Australia, with men hanging out together in one group while women gravitate to another area.

However, Mona also understands that this argument can only go so far: the difference between Iraq and Australia is that in the latter, at some point the two groups can come together to socialise and not feel that they have breached a religious position. In more traditional or conservative families in Iraq, meanwhile, a woman would be looked down upon and her reputation might even be brought into question if she was found sitting among men.

Mona finds that she can easily shift between sitting in a room full of women at her parents' home to mixing with both genders in her own apartment or at work. She is able to handle the contradictions between these scenarios, and can easily adapt her expectations. When she travels on the train to her city office, sits at her desk or orders lunch at a cafe, for example, Mona's daily experiences are inextricably linked with men, so much so that she often doesn't even notice if the person sitting next to her is a man. Sometimes she finds herself the only woman at meetings.

As societies develop, the mark of how far women have progressed is usually judged by their status in public life. Voting, equal pay and home ownership are examples of some of the rights that were claimed by women in Western societies last century. In Australia, Mona has benefited from hard-fought civil struggles that have improved women's lives, while in Iraq, where she was born, she would have been disadvantaged by many social inequalities. When Islam was founded, it gave women rights that were ahead of the times, but these have not necessarily translated into the daily lives of many Muslim women today.

When she was a teenager, Mona regarded the kitchen in her parents' home as central station for her and her sisters. When they were hosting visitors, as was expected of them as women, it was where they came together to get away from any conversations among their mother's friends that they did not want to be a part of; here they gossiped and strategised, including about when to serve snacks. Often they forgot where they were and got too loud for their father's liking, and the sound of their voices would carry into the men's quarters. Mona's father sometimes got annoyed and would come out of his living room and shush them.

'Women exist in this house too, you know,' she would whisper back at her father. She would never raise her voice, though, or do anything to humiliate him while his friends were sitting nearby.

One of her brothers was sometimes sent to deliver the reprimand, acting as her father's delegate. He would dramatically tell his sisters to keep their voices down, but Mona would use the opportunity to point out the obvious: 'They [the visitors] know we are here because they know it is us girls preparing the food.' She would tease: 'If you don't want us to talk, maybe you should prepare everything yourself.' Her brother disapproved of her attitude, but knew that Mona would never follow through on her threat.

Messages between male and female visitors would also be delivered by Mona and her family. For example, when one of the men was ready to leave, he would organise through Mona's brother—who in turn would seek out Mona—for his wife to meet him outside at a certain time. Once, when her mother's friend was ready to leave, she called her husband's mobile to indicate her intentions, even though he was sitting just a few metres away in the other room.

Mona is sympathetic to why her parents laid out their home in such a way, which respects how their pious visitors want to be hosted. And there are other reasons for the segregated rooms, including preserving modesty so that a woman can move around in her home freely—if she will never encounter a man who is not her husband or an immediate relative, she can remove her hijab.

Mona realises that many of her social experiences growing up were mainly lived among women. As an adult, she has chosen to look beyond the strict religious interpretation of her parents' domestic arrangement to try to identify whether there were any social benefits to segregating the genders. She has many fond memories of spending long periods of quality time with women she considered strong and opinionated. The set-up at home meant that she was able to delve into issues with her mother's female friends, and she had the opportunity to have many robust exchanges with them about topics such as politics and religion. Mona also used her time in the women-only living room to correct any misinformation they may have had about what was happening in Australia, which they usually sourced through hearsay. The women respected Mona for her education and often turned to her for advice about things like legal matters.

But Mona also concedes that her ideas about how she wanted to mix with her own friends at home evolved. When she became engaged to Talal, she seriously struggled with the idea that she would not be able to sit in the same room with him when he visited her at home. Talal, a Shia like her but from a Lebanese-Australian background, did not practise such gender segregation at his family home.

When Mona first explained this restriction to Talal, she had to tell him that her father had specifically requested that he respect the family's position. Talal privately explained to Mona that he felt uneasy about it, but the last thing he wanted to do was upset her parents, especially since they were so welcoming and had started to treat him like a son. So he sat in the men's living area whenever he visited.

It was the opposite experience, however, when Mona and her parents visited Talal's family as they got to know each other. They had one living room in their home and all their visitors sat together.

'My parents respected his family and adapted relatively easily,' Mona remembers.

There was another upside to the arrangement, Mona noted: her parents did not need to update each other in the car on their way home as they had been engaging in the same conversations. Usually in the car after visits to other friends' homes, her parents would take turns sharing the main pieces of news from their respective separate gatherings.

As Mona and Talal's relationship developed, Mona's father began to relax his position towards Talal in his home. He said that if they didn't have any other visitors and one of her brothers was around, then Talal could socalise in the same room as Mona, her mother and sisters.

Both Mona and Talal appreciated the breakthrough.

'Talal hated being in what he called the "men's club" when he visited,' Mona recalls. 'He always said the main point of coming over was to see me, and he would get down about things when he didn't get to do this.'

On some occasions, he spent hours at Mona's place without crossing paths with her. The only time they got to talk was when she walked Talal to his car at the end of a visit.

Mona understood how strongly her father felt about his obligations to his religion and traditions, and she respected him for it.

In keeping with this, when Talal visited her parents to formally ask to marry her, she knew that the request would initially be discussed only by the men from both families. Mona and her mother and sisters kept themselves busy in the kitchen while the men talked in their living room. While the kitchen's proximity to this room allowed for some eaves-dropping, for the first time Mona was stung by how isolating the layout of her family's home could be. As a child, she had never really given much thought about the men sitting sepa-rately from the women. Now that everyone was talking about her life, she felt the separation acutely.

The fact that Mona wanted Talal to speak with her father about marriage already spoke volumes to her family about how she felt about him. Her inability to hear what Talal and her father were saying about her future, however, led to Mona's frustrations rising: 'They were talking about the biggest decision of my life, yet I wasn't even there. I actually didn't want Talal to think that whatever my dad said goes, and I wanted to have a say in the matter. I wanted my voice to be heard and to say things in my way.'

As part of their traditions for marriage, Mona's father would also represent her on key issues that would be negotiated for the Islamic marriage contract, such as the *mahr*. Talal's father would do the same for him. This was a mark of respect for fathers, as it was an acknowledgment that no one was better placed than they to look out for their children's interests.

With the men locked away for over an hour, Mona's mother could see how tense Mona was becoming and pleaded with her to stop hovering. 'Go sit down, your dad will tell you everything,' she tried to comfort her. Mona saw that her mother was in the same predicament, in the dark about the details of the conversation taking place about her daughter's future. Unlike Mona, however, her mother was pleased for her husband to manage the family's affairs because she was confident that he would do the right thing by all of them.

As soon as Talal and his family had left, Mona rushed to her bedroom. Earlier in the day, she had agreed with Talal that he would call her with all the details as soon as he left her house. Her phone had only rung once before Mona answered breathlessly: 'Tell me everything, Talal! What did he say? Don't leave anything out.'

After she finally emerged from her room, Mona's mother advised her to give her father some space: he needed time to consider Talal's proposal. For the time being, Mona would have to be content with Talal's interpretation on how things went, which was generally positive.

Despite her changing attitude, the custom of men-only and women-only gatherings continued at Mona's engagement, in keeping with her conservative family's wishes and to ensure that their more pious relatives and friends could attend. The quid pro quo for Mona—but especially Talal—was that their wedding could be mixed. Since Talal's family was less conservative than Mona's on this issue, it was important to them that all of their invited guests could attend the wedding together. However, they knew this meant that some relatives would decline to attend as they considered it *haram*. Mona couldn't help but feel irked that one of her father's closest friends failed to show up with his family at her wedding because it was open to all.

'I was annoyed because I know that his daughters work with men, so for him to hold on to the segregation idea for my wedding . . . I felt there was a level of hypocrisy there.'

The guests at Mona's wedding danced to traditional Lebanese and Iraqi songs, and Mona and Talal even had a slow dance, one of the many Westernised features of the occasion, along with her white dress. No alcohol was served, in keeping with their religion, and the guests kept a respectful tone throughout the proceedings, including on the dance floor, Mona observed.

In contrast to Mona's story, anecdotal evidence suggests that children of migrants in Western countries such as Australia can be more conservative than their parents about the Islam they practice. Where their parents may have grown up in poor villages or towns in their former homelands and were unlikely to have had the opportunity to finish school, their children have lived their lives in the more liberal West with better access to education and employment. But against the backdrop of increasing tensions worldwide about terror-ism, many younger Muslims in Australia have become more informed than their parents about their religion, and in some cases are taking a harder line on certain issues. Examples of this include mothers who do not wear the hijab but daugh-ters who do, or, as mentioned previously, Muslims who have completed the Hajj pilgrimage at a relatively young age, while their parents are yet to fulfil this obligation.

The social segregation of men and women did not pre-viously feature strongly among these groups in Australia. Few Arab Muslim parents, for example, would have organ-ised segregated weddings when they first came to Australia. Indeed, over the years they would have attended many social events—family barbecues, picnics and community festivals—with both men and women in attendance. Now, however, some watch as their children send out engagement or wedding invitations inscribed with the words, 'Women only'.

After Mona and Talal married, her parents were curious about the living arrangements in her new apartment, and asked whether men and women visitors would sit in the same room. Mona explained her limited options and the need for practicality—she only had one living room in her small apartment, which was all she and Talal could afford. So all her visitors would have to be hosted in the same living room. Yet, even if space had not been an issue, Mona had already agreed with Talal that all of their family and friends would sit together when they visited.

While Mona had never seriously challenged her father about the segregated rooms, now that she was older and could draw on her experiences, including the time she had spent in Talal's family home, she felt that the separate quarters had more to do with culture than being a strict religious rule. She concluded that it was not a position that she wanted to maintain in her new life as a married woman.

In fact, married life presented Mona with the opportunity to see her parents, and her father in particular, in a different light. The stretches of mixed socialisation enabled her to witness a side of his personality she had seen little of before. In the company of other women, she found him warm and engaging. She was also happily surprised by how her mother adapted, since she had spent little time with men outside her immediate family circle.

Of her father, Mona explains: 'I think it has opened him up to seeing the fun side of things. My parents can see that when men and women come together we have interesting conversations. They can also see that I have fun with my husband and there isn't a barrier between us.'

Mona still expects her guests to maintain a level of decorum, especially in her father's presence, as she does not want to give him any reason to be offended by the way she is living. 'The gatherings at my place are casual events where everyone is interacting. It makes me happy to see that my dad actually enjoys himself when he comes over.'

7

Good mourning

In the four months after her husband died, Nasreen only left her house for an extended period on three occasions—to attend her son's preschool graduation; his first day at kindergarten; and her father's funeral.

Most people don't prepare for death, but what Nasreen felt even more unready for were the rules and rituals that came with being a female Muslim widow.

Previously, when Nasreen had mourned for relatives from her Lebanese-Australian family, she usually attended a prayer session at a community hall or local mosque, where a sheikh recited from the Quran. This marked a very different send-off to an Anglo-Australian funeral service or wake. The way these funerals were described to her, they were more like celebrations. Nasreen discovered that things were more complicated for a Muslim widow in mourning.

She was only 29 when her husband died in a car accident. From the moment they were informed of the tragedy, his family and relatives swung into action, appealing to hospital authorities for his body to be released as quickly as possible so that he could be buried within 24 hours of his death, as Islamic custom dictates that a body must be buried as quickly as possible after death.

Nasreen endured the first day of mourning at the home of her parents-in-law, which was bursting with so many mourners that some were forced to stand. Muslims take very seriously the duty to pay their respects to the family of the deceased. The dramatic way in which Nasreen's husband had died meant that news of his death spread quickly through the community. She arrived at her in-laws' home early in the morning and did not leave until late that night. The flow of visitors was relentless, and Nasreen had to acknowledge each and every one of the women in attendance. The men sat in separate quarters outside.

When a Muslim dies, the duration of mourning varies. Muslims are technically only expected to mourn for three days following the death of a relative other than a husband. Of course, most people take longer—often 40 days—more for cultural reasons than as a religious requirement. Muslims believe that death is God's way, and the short timeframe of the official mourning period is to motivate individuals to move on with their lives, as they will hopefully be reunited with their loved one in the afterlife.

Nasreen understood that certain customs must be observed while mourning her husband. As part of the mourning process, widows are expected to undertake a period of 'waiting'—called *iddah*—which should consist of four lunar months and ten days, totalling roughly one hundred and thirty days. This expectation is in place primarily to ensure that the father of any child produced after the husbands' death be known. Should the widow know she was pregnant at the time of her husband's death, the *iddah* would last until the end of her pregnancy. As discussed earlier, Islam is fierce on the notion that every child in the Muslim community is born knowing the identity of their father, thereby protecting lineage, avoiding intermarriage and ensuring a woman's modesty against defamation.

During her *iddah*, a Muslim woman is also not allowed to make any arrangements for marriage or wear anything overly decorative.

The *iddah* applies to women not only after the death of a husband, but also after a divorce. For a divorced Muslim woman, the prescribed *iddah* is three months (unless, once again, she is pregnant).

During any *iddah*—for a widow or divorcee—a woman may not remarry.

The notion of an extended period alone after the death of a husband is, of course, nothing new and Muslims are not alone in having established rituals like *iddah*. During Victorian times in Anglo-Saxon countries, for example, a widow was expected to mourn her husband for two years. In ancient China, a straw hut was reportedly built beside a husband's grave so his widow could live there for three years.

The longer she spent at her in-laws that first day, the more anxious Nasreen became. She knew that she was being overly sensitive, but she felt self-conscious about the way she was being watched. Pity permeated the lounge room where she sat among the female mourners; the men headed for the backyard to take their place among the rows of plastic chairs that had been set up on a large patch of grass. As the women whispered their commiserations, Nasreen strained to hear the sheikh's recital of Quranic verses through the crowd of men.

Nasreen was now a single mother to a young child. *Why has my child been left without a father?* she asked Allah. *Why do I have to be a widow at such a young age? Why did my husband have to die?*

She found herself struggling to make sense of it all. Nasreen did not feel that she was going to get the spiritual support that she needed, and being away from her own home and its familiar comforts was not helping matters.

In need of some respite, Nasreen went into a bedroom and called a sheikh whose advice she valued. She explained that she wanted his guidance on the *iddah*, as she needed to know what it would mean for her life on a practical level. The sheikh explained that under the *iddah*, it is forbidden for a woman to spend the night outside her own home—that is, the home she shared with her husband—except for a legitimate reason such as an eviction or fearing for her safety. Nasreen could not see how such scenarios applied to her, especially since she lived in her own home and her family had asked one of her brothers to move in with her until she got back on her feet.

After speaking to the sheikh, Nasreen was convinced that *iddah* would be the first step in a new, strong and successful life for her and her son now that her husband was gone. After all the drama, Nasreen was actually looking forward to spending more time on her own at home and finding her strength again.

'I was at my in-laws, looked into my son's eyes and realised that I needed to do this, I needed to do the *iddah*,' Nasreen recalls. 'I left their place and couldn't wait to get home. I was going to start a new life and I felt the only way I could do that was to strengthen my faith by fulfilling the *iddah*.'

During her *iddah*, Nasreen would be expected to follow some strict guidelines. The next several months would test her faith.

Not everyone supported Nasreen's decision to observe the *iddah*—in fact, she didn't know any other woman who had observed it—and the resistance came from unexpected quarters.

Her brother, who Nasreen was getting used to having around, understood why she was doing it. But just a few weeks in, other family members became concerned about how strict she was being on herself. They told Nasreen that they didn't think she needed to prove her devotion to her husband or religion by committing to stay home for such a long time. They believed that, had she lived in a Muslim society where Islamic rules are followed, things would be different. Since she lived in Australia and was expected to take care of her child and run her home, they weren't convinced that she had to fulfil the whole *iddah*.

For women like Nasreen, however, observing the *iddah* even in a non-Islamic country is their way of demonstrating the depth of their faith and the extent of their mourning. Nasreen concedes that she was also conscious of avoiding any aspersions that might otherwise be cast upon her character, as many would expect that someone in her position would indeed mourn for a long time. However, she acknowledges that the length of the *iddah* is a big ask—for anyone. She knows some people struggle with the notion of having to stay home even for just one day.

Nasreen braced herself for a steady stream of female visitors looking to fulfil the Islamic custom of bringing their condolences in person. Their husbands would offer the same sentiments at her in-laws' house because it would not be acceptable for a man to enter her home if she did not have a *mahram* with her. No man outside her immediate family could enter her home while her *mahram*—in Nasreen's case, her brother—was away.

During her first full week at home for the *iddah*, Nasreen hardly had any time to herself. She practically lived on her sofa, dressed in dark clothes, ready to receive mourners. Some of them were extremely curious about her decision to undertake the *iddah*. Would this young woman be strong enough, respectful enough, Muslim enough, to observe the whole period of the *iddah*? Surely young, modern women like Nasreen with myriad responsibilities in the real world did not have the patience to complete it?

But Nasreen was adamant.

Nasreen learned that important concessions for a woman undertaking the *iddah* can be approved by a sheikh on a case-by-case basis. This is because Islam recognises that each woman's particular circumstances must be taken into account. For example, if she needed to see a doctor, attend classes or shop for necessities, then she should be able to do all of these things, so long as she performed them during the day and returned home before nightfall.

To truly respect the process, however, Nasreen felt that she needed to stay home pretty much all of the time. She did not want to be tempted by everyday life and wanted to take the time to be closer to Allah; staying home meant that she could achieve these things. As her brother had already moved in, she knew she could rely on him to run her errands and help with dropping off and picking up her son from school, so there was no need for her to venture out unless for important milestones or an emergency. However, if something urgent came up, she took a sensible approach and reassessed the situation, and on those few occasions, Nasreen was careful to remain modest and went about her life in public in a quiet manner.

Nasreen's run of misfortune continued when her father died not long after she lost her husband, a predicament which only made her more determined to keep faith with the *iddah*. This, despite the fact that, unlike Nasreen, it didn't take long for her husband's family and her mother to get on with their lives. She tried not be judgmental, but it was hard not to notice how quickly they returned to their regular routines. Nasreen hoped that the respect she had shown them would be recipro-cated—for them to understand why she had chosen to spend a third of the year practically confined to her home. Instead, her in-laws tried to pressure her to break the *iddah*. Nasreen resisted, but understood what they were most worried about was the lack of time they were spending with their grandchild as Nasreen did not want to venture out herself.

She was also mature enough to understand that everyone dealt with grief differently. Many who have suffered a huge personal loss put their energy into something new in order to move on. However, Nasreen knew that she would not be able to simply go about her life as before.

As the days at home turned into weeks and months, Nasreen found herself declining invitations from her friends for coffee, dinner or the movies. Some seemed to think that because Nasreen was young, her commitment would soon wane. But Nasreen found that it wasn't as hard as she had thought it would be to decline these requests and, after a while, her friends stopped asking. It wasn't like Nasreen didn't miss going out. She did. Indeed, the *iddah* made her realise how much she appreciated her friends and what it meant to have the freedom to go out and have a good time. For now, however, the *iddah* came first.

Nasreen took each day as it came—her husband's sudden death forced her to no longer look too far ahead. She spent her days contemplating, praying and spending quality time with her child. Being at home for an extended period also heightened Nasreen's senses. She now took the time to listen to the birds chirping every morning in the trees outside her bedroom window, to smell the jasmine flowering in her back garden and to enjoy the taste of her freshly brewed coffee.

At times, Nasreen was tempted to cave, to stop the *iddah*. During these challenging moments, she built up her strength by looking for answers in the Quranic scriptures to help her make sense of what she was going through.

Many times she felt negative emotions: fear (for her future and her child); anguish (for what her child would miss out on by not having a father); and sadness (for wasting time worrying about the small things). But the more time she spent immersing herself in the scriptures of the Quran, the more she felt at peace. Writing about her feelings also helped: 'The sorrow haunts me, but I read the Quran to search for answers within the meaningful verses.'

While busy people everywhere complain about wanting to jump off life's treadmill and take some time out, the *iddah* afforded Nasreen the chance to do just that, though she was also aware that she did not have a job to keep up. She firmly believes, though, that performing the *iddah* gave her the time to reflect away from all the hustle and bustle. She certainly believes that it brought her closer to Allah and that being able to take the time to properly mourn her husband had a positive impact on her mental health. As she had the time to put real thought into every action, it meant that everything soon took on a new significance.

'I really believe that if I hadn't removed myself from my busy life, the whole experience of losing my husband would have been even more negative, especially in the early days of mourning.'

Ten days before the official end of the *iddah*, Nasreen had an important decision to make. When she moved to Australia as a teenager, she dreamed of going to university and getting a job in the IT industry. She did well at school for someone who was still relatively new to the country and was proud of having gained a place at university. Her studies, however, were interrupted—first by her engagement and then marriage followed by pregnancy.

After getting a small taste of what life is like on welfare payments following her husband's death, Nasreen knew that, if she had any hope of a better future for herself and her child, she needed to go to university. This was what was driving her now.

Once again, she turned to her sheikh for advice: could she leave her house a week or so before the end of the *iddah* so that she could go back to university at the start of the semester? It was important to her sense of balance to start her classes on time. Fortunately, the sheikh shared Nasreen's view that attending university had become a necessity for her future prospects, and agreed she could end the *iddah* a little earlier.

'I felt that, because I had done my duty towards Allah with the *iddah*, I was ready to tackle the world and overcome any hardship that would be thrown at me,' Nasreen confides. 'It was like the world was opening its arms to me . . .'

When Nasreen stepped outside her front door for the first time in four months as a woman no longer under *iddah*, she felt her outlook on life was unmistakably positive. Arriving at her university lecture, she took her seat, turned to the woman sitting next to her and smiled. It was a good morning.

8

Fostering love

'There is no adoption in Islam.'

Majida delivers these words without emotion.

Her expression of this hardline religious position on adoption, however, has not stopped Majida from caring for children who were not born to her. While she chooses to never legally adopt a child due to her religion, Majida explains that she can still foster a child.

The leading advocate for this is the Prophet Muhammad himself, who fostered a young boy and treated him as though he were his own son.

Therefore, caring for a child, including one that is orphaned, is very much encouraged among Muslims. However, it must be explicitly acknowledged that they are not your biological offspring. This is because the Quran has strict rules about the legal relationship between a child and the family caring for him or her, and the Islamic position is that a child must be named after their biological father only. This was particularly relevant in Arabian cultures, where children were literally named 'son of' or 'daughter of' their father—'Ali ibn Abu Talib' translates as 'Ali, son of Abu Talib'. According to Islamic adoption laws, then, if Ali had been adopted by a man named Muhammad, his name could not be changed to 'Ali ibn Muhammad'; he must retain the name of his biological father. Muslim children must always have the right to paternity. Ultimately, this means they cannot be deprived of their rightful inheritance, as Islam forbids a father from disinheriting his natural children.

Majida was in her mid thirties and already had three young children of her own when she decided to explore the idea of foster care. Her husband had died some years earlier and she had no desire to remarry. She was particularly keen for her young daughter Yasmeen to be around children closer to her age, especially after it became obvious that her sons were more interested in playing together than with their little sister, whose father had died when she was aged only two.

When Majida migrated to Australia from Lebanon aged nineteen in the late 1980s to marry her husband, she came alone and had no immediate family here. The product of a strict upbringing, she had worn the hijab since she was fifteen.

But her new husband, who had an Arab Muslim background and grew up in Australia, had other ideas. He did not want his young wife to wear the head covering. Her husband's views came as a surprise to the devout Majida, who would go on to have many arguments with him about it.

When the issue threatened to end their relationship, Majida turned to her parents in Lebanon. Far away from their daughter and fearing for her future, they advised her to put her marriage ahead of the hijab. Their advice came as yet another shock as Majida had thought they would side with her given their piousness.

'They said they didn't want me to ruin my life,' Majida says of her family's advice.

For a long time after making the painful decision to remove her hijab, Majida says she felt naked without it. 'I grew up with every woman in my family wearing it. It turned out that my husband didn't want to be with a woman in a headscarf. He wanted someone like me from Lebanon who was a virgin in every way, but here in Australia he also wanted me to look a certain way.'

When her husband died, Majida was only 28. She put the hijab back on and started to meet new people. Majida also had a strong desire to give back to the community. She had no idea that in such a wealthy country like Australia there could be children in dire circumstances. She was brought up in a much poorer society where she had never met any adopted or fostered children. In many Muslim communities, the extended family is typically very strong, and so it would be highly unusual for a child to be without a close relative to care for them. Very few children would therefore need to be taken in by a stranger and removed from their cultural and religious roots.

'I thought people living in Australia would have a better life than where I came from. I asked, *Can there really be parents who don't want their children?*'

After successfully applying to be a foster carer, Majida hoped for a little girl to come into her family's life. The idea of fostering a baby did not appeal to her, because she didn't want to change nappies again or have to wake in the middle of the night for feeds. But Majida was quickly informed that she could not pick and choose. Those requiring support tended to be in acute need and she would be called upon to take in whoever was deemed to be in most need of her support.

The government agency with whom Majida was dealing had to understand that, because she was a Muslim, there were certain aspects of her and her children's lives that would not change with a foster child around. One of the things she came to appreciate most about the process was just how much her own children's feelings were taken into account by her case worker. If her children, for example, did not feel comfortable with any part of the process, their views were respected.

Majida was careful not to force her ways on to any foster child, not that she would have been allowed to do so as her activities were carefully monitored. As a practising Muslim, however, she would pray when it was time to do so, and regularly performed this ritual with her young children. If it was Ramadan, she (and her children as they got older) would abstain from food and drink during daylight hours.

'I knew these children would come to us having had a different upbringing,' Majida explains, 'but I needed to make sure that my children's lives were not changed as well.'

Majida's desire to nurture another child was put to the test when the first child placed in her care was a newborn. It was an emergency situation. Majida was informed that the boy's mother had a Cambodian background, while his father was of Lebanese heritage. Neither parent was in a position to care for the baby, least of all the mother who had a drug problem.

After five months with her family, the little boy was fostered out again to a childless woman from an Iraqi background. 'She was crazy about him and wanted to keep him forever,' Majida says of the baby's second foster mother.

The two foster parents became friendly after Majida was required to visit the boy daily for two weeks at his new home to help him settle in to the different environment.

But after just a few weeks, the new foster carer called Majida in tears, repeating over and again, 'They took him'. It turned out that the baby's grandmother on his father's side had not given up on him and wanted to become his carer.

Majida knew exactly what the other foster mother was going through. She and her children had also become attached to the boy even after a short period of time. 'That's the hard thing about being a foster carer; we all got close to him.'

Majida tried to soothe the distraught woman with the same words she had used to comfort herself: 'You are helping these kids and it's better that they grow up with their family.'

On another occasion, Majida was asked to foster a six-and-a-half-year-old girl and her five-year-old brother. They had an Anglo mother and a father with an Arab Muslim background.

Although she was reluctant to look after two at a time, Majida agreed.

On their first night with her family, the boy approached Majida in the kitchen and asked for a ham sandwich. 'That's what my mum gives me,' he said.

As a Muslim, Majida had never brought any pork-based foods into her home—they are prohibited, as pigs are considered unclean animals in Islam. 'I told him that my children eat good food, and he would get the same.'

Meanwhile, the boy's sister ate with the family without any problems and he soon forgot about ham. He also started copying Majida's prayer moves.

'He would ask me about praying, and I would explain that I am a Muslim. But I didn't force anything on him.'

The children's mother was entitled to visit them once a week at the government agency. During one of these visits, she picked her children up after school and had brought them a snack—a burger with bacon. On seeing this, the boy told his mother: 'We don't eat bacon.'

Majida was informed that the mother became angry, questioning the case worker about why her children's eating habits had changed. The mother was told that the children were being well looked after and fed, and that they were not being forced to do or eat anything they didn't want. When the children came into her care, it was explained to Majida that their diet mainly consisted of takeaway meals. At her home, Majida was used to cooking fresh Lebanese food every day, and she could see how well the children were responding to her nutritious dishes.

When her daughter, Yasmeen, was much older, Majida was again asked to care for two children at the same time—sisters, aged eight and twelve. They were from an Arab Muslim background, and Majida admits that knowing they had the same background as her made it easier to agree to the request. She was careful to treat all the children she cared for the same, regardless of their backgrounds, but as a Muslim she couldn't help but feel that she was also doing something religiously positive whenever the foster child shared her religion.

For the first time since becoming a foster parent, however, Majida faced resistance from one of her children. At fifteen, Yasmeen was concerned because the older girl attended her high school and would be travelling on the same bus. She complained that this made her feel as though she had to take responsibility for her.

The case worker was very keen for the girls to live with Majida; she felt it was a good fit. So she organised for Majida and her children to spend some time alone with the girls. If they still felt uncomfortable, Majida was assured that the agency would respect their feelings and find the girls another home.

'They're good kids and I don't want to break them up,' the case worker appealed to Majida, who herself was also concerned about looking after two foster children at once again. At the end of the organised visit, however, Yasmeen was happy enough to agree for the girls to live with her family.

They ended up staying for two years. During this time, the girls regularly visited their older teenage sister, who lived with another family. When she turned eighteen, she went to court to become the legal guardian of her two sisters. All three girls now live together and continue to visit Majida and her children, with whom they have developed a strong bond over the years.

Majida has acted as a foster parent to a total of six children. With her sons and daughter grown and starting their own families, she has been concentrating on helping them establish their adult lives.

Now, at 46, Majida's life has taken an unexpected turn.

One Saturday morning, Anthony knocked on her front door to inquire about the granny flat at the back of her house. A mutual friend, a work colleague, had told him that Majida was looking for a tenant.

After he had inspected the property, Majida offered Anthony a cup of coffee. She thought nothing of this gesture, as Arabs are known for their hospitality. Sitting down together at an outdoor table in her backyard—Majida had to host Anthony in an open area as she could not be alone in her house with a non-*mahram* man—Anthony found it easy to talk to Majida.

He had grown up in Greece and moved to Australia in his early twenties to live with his mother, who he had not seen since she left him and his younger sister as little children with their father.

Now 50, he was divorced and living in his mother's garage as he tried to get back on his feet. His life had taken a series of negative turns and he hoped to save enough money to start afresh. His relationship with his mother had never become a close one, he explained to Majida, although he appreciated that she allowed him, albeit grudgingly, to have a roof over his head. To cause her the least imposition, Anthony had become a paid member of a local club so that he could use their restrooms to shower before returning to his mother's garage at night to sleep.

Majida was shocked at some of the measures Anthony had taken to keep out of his mother's way. She was used to family members helping each other out, as many people from Arab backgrounds believe it is their duty to do so.

While she felt sorry for Anthony after hearing about his troubles, he missed out on the rental as he was not in a position to take it immediately and Majida was keen to find a tenant quickly.

❖

Months after his visit, Anthony contacted Majida again through their mutual friend.

'I didn't even really remember what he looked like,' she says.

Yet Anthony remembered her well. He wanted to get to know her—and not as a tenant.

In the eighteen years since her husband had died, Majida had fielded several offers of marriage, usually orchestrated by her girlfriends. She was always adamant that she didn't want a man to interfere in her children's lives as they were growing up. Her eldest was only seven when his father died, and Majida did not like the thought of another man telling him what to do.

At first, Majida strongly resisted Anthony's advances. She knew he wasn't a Muslim and so didn't want to waste her time thinking about him. But the mutual friend encouraged her to give Anthony a chance. He explained that he had advised Anthony that if he was genuinely interested in her, then he would need to read up on the basics of Islam as Majida was a practising Muslim and wouldn't want to be with someone who didn't share her values.

Despite Majida's obvious reluctance, Anthony persisted. After several failed attempts, he finally convinced her to meet him for a coffee. Soon, they were regularly spending time together and Majida began to look forward to seeing him. She did not change her lifestyle—instead she went about her life as normal, which included attending weekly religious classes. Majida mentioned these sessions to Anthony while discussing their schedules and he asked if he could join her at one of her classes. After this gesture, which Majida believed was made out of genuine interest, she started to think that Anthony was getting to know Islam for the right reasons.

Only three months after they first got together, Anthony told Majida that he was ready to take the *Shahada*, the expression of faith for Muslims. Majida was excited about Anthony's decision and attended a small ceremony with him at a mosque, where he received a certificate to new Muslims which read: 'Certification of Islam. This is to certify that Anthony has taken the declaration and testified that there is no God worthy of worship except Allah and that Muhammad (peace be upon him) is His servant and final Messenger and to fulfil the five pillars of Islam.' The certificate was dated and signed by two witnesses.

Soon afterwards, Majida and Anthony married.

During the months they had been getting to know each other, Anthony never saw Majida without her hijab. Unlike her first husband, Anthony had no problem with the head covering. Muslim women in hijab like Majida can only remove it in the presence of their husband or close family members. After their small wedding, when they were alone, Anthony saw her hair for the first time.

Initially, Majida was nervous about telling her family in Lebanon about Anthony, and was relieved at how easy it was to gain their acceptance, which was very important to her.

'I thought it would be a hard idea for them to accept as they are very traditional, but my father said, "Why not? Is he a Muslim? You are not young and you have nothing to lose".'

It took a little longer to convince her children, who had some concerns about Anthony's motives. But they too have since come around to the idea—and in so doing, followed in their mother's footsteps in caring for someone who has come into their family as an outsider.

Majida is not completely closed off to fostering again—her contact details remain with the agency—but she is now busy with her own life in a different way.

'I was young when my husband died—I could've just looked after myself. But fostering a child is about showing humanity and my children got to see that there are kids out there who don't have parents. They appreciate me more because of that.'

9

A temporary act

Rania had two stipulations for her 'husband', Imad: he would not live with her and they would break up in a month's time.

When they met, both in their late twenties, there was no established procedure in their world for the boyfriend/girlfriend relationship that they began to enjoy. The traditional Western concept of dating is at odds with the strict rules of courtship in Islam and Rania's Islamic values put her under pressure to conduct her relationship with Imad in a way that was religiously acceptable.

So she asked him to meet her at a cafe to discuss their future. She wanted to talk about where things were heading and to suggest that, if they were to continue seeing each other, she wanted to be in a temporary Islamic marriage (*mut'ah*) with him.

Both she and Imad were Shia Muslims from Iraqi backgrounds. Unlike Rania, this would be Imad's first experience of a fixed, short-term marriage. Rania had done her homework and understood that all that was required for the *mut'ah* was a verbal agreement about the terms of the arrangement, which was designed to protect their rights, including in the event that Rania got pregnant and paternity became an issue.

The specific details came down to their own expectations, including how long the relationship should last and Rania's *mahr*. The set-up could be for as short or as long as they agreed, even a day if that was what they both wanted. No official paperwork or filing of documents was necessary.

After leaving the cafe together and having agreed on the *mut'ah* and its terms, Rania got into Imad's car and the two exchanged vows as they sat in the dark. No witnesses were necessary, except Allah.

Rania: 'I give myself to you to marry for the discussed dowry and the discussed date.'

Imad: 'I agree to the marriage.'

They then kissed.

Rania and Imad had pronounced much the same words that Muslim couples would exchange in front of a sheikh. Imad had agreed to Rania's request for the short-term marriage to be set for one month. At the end of that period, they would either call things off or renew the verbal contract depending on how they felt about each other.

Rania was first married at the age of fifteen to Hussein—who was twelve years older and grew up in Iraq before becoming a refugee as an adult.

Her family in Australia—the two brothers with whom she lived in Sydney—had pushed for the marriage. She knew they were relieved to marry her off because, in wanting to continue her education, Rania had become quite a handful (her brothers' words, not hers). She was married under Islamic law, which meant no marriage certificate was lodged with the Australian authorities (the sheikh was very careful about this point, Rania recalls).

Her brothers, relatively new to Australia and with conservative views from Iraq that a girl should marry young, had not known how to handle what they considered to be Rania's rebellion. To further encourage the marriage, they promised that Hussein would support her dreams. This is a line that is sold to many girls with Rania's background: that being married will somehow lead to more independence and opportunities such as attending university. But in many cases, the girl becomes a woman, a wife, a mother and finally her dreams for something more become just that—a dream.

Rania and Hussein married not long after he came to Australia. He was very conservative and well-versed in the teachings of the Quran; family and friends regularly turned to him for religious advice. After a few years, Rania could see that Hussein was struggling with his new life in Australia. He often talked about how he missed his family back in Iraq and how Australia was never meant to be a long-term proposition for him. On top of this difficulty, Rania never felt religious enough for him and questioned their relationship. All the while, she continued to think about going to university.

Women in Rania's position are often warned they have more to lose from a relationship ending, and her brothers echoed these sentiments, regularly threatening her: 'Do you think anyone is going to marry you if you are a divorced woman?' In many Arab communities, a Muslim woman's behaviour or chastity is tied to male honour. Rania's brothers took this hard-line position as they thought her relationship with Hussein also reflected on their reputation.

Rania was especially worried that if she agreed to visit Iraq with Hussein as he had often suggested, even for a short trip, he would make it difficult for her return to Australia and to divorce, as their old homeland was still a conservative country when it came to marriage and children. They now had a young child, Kasim, and women could lose custody of their children under the religious rules there.

Rania could think of nothing worse than returning to Iraq at this point in her life. She had carved out a small amount of happiness and independence living in Australia, and continued to resist Hussein's calls for them to pack up their lives and move back overseas. And she was aware that it wasn't all about her anymore: Rania wanted to give Kasim a better life than the one she knew he would have in Iraq.

Eventually, it became clear that Rania and Hussein couldn't reconcile their differences. Their views about the future were too different, and Rania was no longer able to stand his negativity about living in Australia. Looking back on the relationship now, Rania says she knew from the first week of meeting Hussein that he was not right for her. Even during their engagement, she had tried to break things off.

Although he had finally got to the point where he too didn't want to continue their marriage, it took Rania another year and a half to convince Hussein to divorce her Islamically before he left for Iraq and to accept that their child should stay with her in Australia.

When things finally ended, she says she and Hussein divorced over the phone.

When this was all concluded, Rania found herself a single mother, determined to show her son that she could give him a good life. She successfully enrolled in a course at university, and earned some extra money in her spare time tutoring young students in Arabic, in which she was fluent.

After her divorce, Rania's social life had shrunk considerably. She was upset that in some quarters, her divorced lifestyle had become the subject of gossip and she found it best to withdraw from some of her friendships.

For the first few years after Hussein left, Rania devoted all her time to her studies and her son, trying to build their lives again. One night, restless about her future and missing the company of adults, Rania turned to an online forum for some conversation. Soon enough, she was talking to several men with Arab backgrounds about her life, sharing songs and even exchanging poems.

After a few weeks one of her online friends, Ahmad, invited her for a coffee. He ended up being her first *mut'ah* relationship after her divorce from Hussein.

Though she felt as though this was the first time she had been in love, right from the start Rania knew that she did not want to commit herself to a full marriage. She wanted to be in a relationship with a man but to do things the right way under Islamic rules—that is, to be married to the person with whom she was being intimate—yet she didn't want to think of things as being forever.

This was when she thought of *mut'ah*—she had heard stories about Muslim men and women having religiously appropriate relationships as part of a temporary marriage.

'I never wanted a divorce on my back in the first place, and I know that a second marriage can break a person just as much, so,' Rania decided, 'short-term Islamic marriages are the path for me.'

Since Rania had been in a full marriage before, her *mut'ah* with Ahmad did not require her father's knowledge or approval, as it would have if it had been her first marriage. She did not mention the *mut'ah* to her brothers, either, who would never understand. More than anything, she was afraid of their judgment and reaction.

While anecdotally a growing number of young Muslim men in Australia—mainly from the Shia branch—are practising short-term marriages, Rania knew her brothers would be firmly opposed to the idea. They would be particularly concerned about what other people would say about her morals. Rania herself was acutely aware of being in the minority with her views on *mut'ah* relationships, and was worried about being called a loose woman if it became widely known that she was involved with men under these circumstances.

Eventually, things with Ahmad came to an end, but Rania was convinced she was Islamically within her rights to take part in other *mut'ah*.

At the cafe with Imad, it was the thought of what to do about her *mahr* that had occupied her mind more than the length of the actual arrangement, since Rania was determined not to feel as though she was a kept woman. These feelings stemmed from her marriage to Hussein. He had been the breadwinner while Rania stayed home to care for Kasim. She felt the financial inequality was used against her as she always had to ask for money to purchase basic items and account for every dollar.

Hussein would also use the *mahr* he had agreed upon at their marriage against her, constantly reminding her how it included a significant amount of gold jewellery, as is the custom in Middle Eastern communities. While Rania appreciated the jewellery, she felt it owned her because she never had the freedom to do with it as she pleased.

With Imad, Rania did not request a full *mahr* as part of the *mut'ah*; instead, she decided to ask for some fine chocolates. Imad was more than happy to oblige. When challenged later by a friend about whether she should have asked for more, Rania stressed that she didn't want to feel owned by a man or that she owed him anything, as she had with Hussein, and was more than satisfied with the chocolates.

Rania was relieved when all the key details were sorted with Imad. She knew exactly what she wanted—although she didn't find it easy discussing such pragmatic matters, she compared working through the details of the relationship to the 'money talk' that many couples have at some point in their relationship.

After things were settled, Rania decided to share the news of their arrangement with a few of her close girlfriends. She was confident about the decision she had taken with Imad and was a little surprised when she received some mixed reactions. A couple of Rania's friends expressed their concerns about the relationship as they did not judge Imad to be a committed Muslim, which made them question his intentions with Rania and whether he was entitled to benefit from the *mut'ah* set-up in the first place.

One friend, Widad, was particularly vocal in these views, as she was not convinced at all of Imad's motives. Rania's modest *mahr* particularly irked Widad because she thought it showed how little Imad thought of her friend, even though the chocolates had been Rania's idea.

To Rania, Imad was one of the most generous men she had met; when they went out, he always paid for their meals and entertainment. Besides, as she explained to Widad, the idea of a traditional marriage scared her more than being short-changed on the *mahr* with Imad: 'All I want is to not be in something that I can't get out of quickly if I want to.'

Imad was so happy with her that, after a month, he brought up the idea of getting married the 'real way'. Rania was enjoying her relationship with him, but quickly brushed off the idea. She was adamant that she wasn't ready for all the demands of a full marriage. Instead, she kept agreeing to renew her temporary relationship with Imad, asking for more time so they could keep getting to know one another.

After educating herself about the rights of women in a short-term Islamic marriage, Rania understood that at the end of each agreed-upon period, she would have to renew her vows, if she so desired. In the months that followed, Rania continued to renew her vows with Imad every month. As the renewal date approached, she would remind him: 'It's coming, it's tomorrow, let's do it again.' Sometimes, she would joke: 'I only want to renew it for a week.'

Without this verbal contract in place, Imad could not see Rania without her hijab. Once, when they were running late for renewing their vows, Imad was forced to stand behind a wall in Rania's apartment and confirm the arrangement before he could see her again without her hijab.

One month with Imad turned into three years and Rania was starting to think that perhaps they were ready to marry the way Imad had suggested early on. She had fallen in love, and Kasim had also developed a close bond with him.

However, an important piece of the relationship puzzle was missing: Rania had never met Imad's family and she now learned that they had a problem with him pursuing a full marriage with a divorced woman. The issue began to fester between them, and Rania questioned whether Imad really accepted her for who she was. When he suggested for a second time that they get married, all Rania could think about was his family's disapproval. On hearing that he couldn't convince even his younger sister to meet her, Rania became distraught.

'Let's get married anyway,' Imad pleaded with her.

'I haven't been with you for the past three years to get married like a thief,' she snapped.

Another friend had bluntly warned Rania not to expect too much from Muslim men who were involved in a temporary marriage, a message that came back to haunt her: 'If your son's own father abandoned him, and didn't accept his responsibilities, what is going to make another Arab man come in and take on that responsibility?' Rania had argued with her friend that she knew quite a few men who had no problem caring for children who weren't their own.

In the early days of her relationship with Imad, Rania had met with him away from Kasim. As their relationship became more serious, though, Imad began to visit her apartment while Kasim was at home. Rania knew it was very likely that Kasim would eventually develop a father–son relationship with Imad, especially since his own father was no longer in his life. When they went on a skiing holiday together, Rania said that it felt like they were a family. It is a memory that she continues to hold on to.

Rania's friend Widad was still angry with her, as she felt Rania had allowed herself to be exploited, and, to some in the community, was engaging in a form of prostitution.

Widad, a Shia like Rania, has noticed a recent uptake in *mut'ah* among Iraqi-Australians. One of her brothers divulged that a few sheikhs in Sydney are counselling young Muslim men, even via Facebook, to attend to their desires in this way. Apparently, the sheikhs feel that it is a better option than turning to pornography or brothels.

Widad does not suggest that the interest in *mut'ah* is one-sided—'Women want it too'—but the informal nature of a temporary set-up means that no one really knows how many of these unions are taking place.

The experience is thought to be especially popular among the younger generation of Shias in Australia, who want to respect their religious beliefs against the backdrop of a Western lifestyle. They are adopting the ancient practice in the belief that it means they are not violating Sharia, which does not approve of sex outside of marriage.

The practice is divided along Muslim branch lines. While both Shias and Sunnis practise informal marriages, they are arguably more prevalent in the Shia community, which reportedly states practitioners are simply following the Quran. Sunnis generally acknowledge that historically, people have engaged in a legal 'traveller's marriage' when away for long stretches on business, but they insist that temporary marriage was later banned in Islam. Some scholars, while not condoning it, argue that the Sunni traveller's marriage was not strictly temporary anyway, as the intention was one of permanence.

Unfortunately, in the end, Rania's relationship with Imad did not survive. He disappeared not just from her life, but also Kasim's, who sadly asked Rania: 'Is he coming back?'

When she reflects on her life, Rania thinks her attitude towards men has been affected by her parents' divorce. They broke up when the family lived in Iraq and she was five, the youngest child.

Rania has learned that divorce was uncommon in Iraq in those days, and her older brothers and sisters later told her that the family's reputation suffered as a result. But they also spoke of some of the good times they had as a family growing up, when her parents were still together and they would enjoy summer trips to Iraq's mountainous north for the cooler weather.

'As for me, I only remember my parents fighting and the long stretches I had to spend alone outside,' Rania sighs.

She does not have happy memories of her mother, and in fact has never really had a relationship with her, as she still lives in Iraq.

After her mother left (following an affair with a cousin), Rania was raised by one of her older sisters until that sister got married. Then another sister took on the role.

This second sister was young herself at the time, and more interested in talking to the boy next door. Rania recalls playing messenger for them. They would write letters to each other and she and her little cousin were responsible for delivering them. It was fun, until Rania's brothers found out and started beating her sister. Their father wasn't at home a lot of the time, so the brothers felt they had the authority to do anything. Rania was beaten too, for delivering the mail.

Meanwhile, Rania's father had remarried. She remembers him going away to sleep at a hotel overnight with his new bride and thinks that was the first time he had ever left them alone at night. Rania didn't like it.

Her father's second wife was middle-aged and pious. This was her first marriage. Rania remembers that she was short and petite, just as her own mother had been. Her father used to crudely joke that all his wives were short so that when they carried his coffin, it wouldn't be unbalanced.

This second marriage did not last long. Rania remembers his wife's sister and her husband came over one night to help pack her belongings. They even unscrewed the chandelier in her father's bedroom, a gift the newlyweds had received upon their wedding. After she left, her father kept bringing up the scene with the chandelier, which he could not get over. Apparently her stepmother left because she couldn't handle looking after Rania's teenage brothers, a duty expected of second wives. Rania doesn't blame her for that: 'They are your typical Middle Eastern entitled boys who think they need to be served at all times.'

Despite the many upheavals in her life, Rania always felt that her father looked out for her. When she was little, he made sure he always had lollies in his pocket when he came home. She has fond memories of sitting on his lap and letting him play with her hair.

❖

Rania has tried to reach out to her mother. When she visited Iraq a few years ago, she attempted to arrange several meetings in Karbala, where her mother lives, but Rania says that each time her mother had an excuse for not showing.

During a phone call while still in Iraq, her mother scolded her for the amount of time she was spending with one of her sisters, who also lives in Iraq.

'She kind of did raise me,' Rania explained.

Her mother was not impressed: 'Really? So she changed your nappies and woke up in the night to feed you?'

It is hard for Rania and her siblings to understand their mother's attitude towards her, since her mother has relationships with the rest of the children, albeit not strong ones. The only difference that Rania can explain between her and her brothers and sisters is that she is the only child who does not support her mother financially. As a single parent in Australia putting herself through university, Rania has little money to spare. 'When other people come from Australia, they usually have money,' her mother has pointed out.

It is little spoken of, but many a village or town across the Middle East is sustained by family members in countries like

Australia sending money back to their relatives, many of whom would find it hard to get by without such financial support. On the flip-side, some migrants to Australia have been known to complain that their families in their native homelands have little understanding of just how hard they work to make ends meet. Some put it this way: 'They think because we live in Australia, we are rich. But they don't know that we work from morning until night to make money and pay our bills. Money does not grow on trees here.'

For now, Rania thinks that she has done all she can to try to have a relationship with her mother. 'Even one of my brothers, who never defends me about anything, thinks it's weird the way she is with me and shrugs his shoulders at her behaviour.'

Perhaps things will change if Rania follows through on her last message to her mother: 'When I finish university and start to work, I will send you money.'

After her experience of *mut'ah* with Ahmad and Imad, Rania was involved in a third one. But her time with Mustafa was very much in keeping with the intended short nature of such a relationship—six months. She was grateful that she could end things without too much hassle.

Rania has decided that this third go at a short-term marriage will be her last, at least for a while. She has not changed her mind about the *mut'ah*, but has come to realise that even with such temporary arrangements an enormous amount of time, effort and emotional energy is inevitably expended.

She now wants to take some time to think about what kind of a relationship she really wants, and is even prepared to contemplate a permanent marriage again without the need for a *mut'ah*.

'At 34, I've had four relationships, but none turned into a happily ever after.'

10

You don't look like a Muslim

'You're a Muslim?'

Samreena is no longer surprised by this reaction, as she is used to the idea that most people's perception of a Muslim woman is of one wearing a hijab.

A perfect example of this misconception, she explains, took place at work. 'I was with a co-worker and I had to tell him I was fasting; it was just randomly brought up . . . I can't remember how, and his reaction was, "What, you're Muslim? I had no idea, wow".'

His words were delivered more with disbelief than simple surprise, Samreena recalls. When she asked why he didn't think she would be a Muslim, he replied: 'You don't have that headscarf on. Plus, you don't act like it.'

The last part of his comment intrigued Samreena. 'What's "acting" like a Muslim?' she queried.

Before her colleague had a chance to respond, however, Samreena found herself answering her own question: 'As a matter of fact, I *do* act like a Muslim . . . I pray during the day in one of our meeting rooms. Didn't you know that?'

Her colleague was taken aback.

'I think his idea of a Muslim woman,' Samreena says, 'is someone . . . who doesn't openly talk to men the way I was doing with him. I assured him that Muslim women are free to talk to men, and can be friendly about it, and that there are many of us Muslims who don't wear the hijab.'

Samreena knows that she is not the first person to be judged on her looks—her colleague's attitude exemplified a stereotype about Muslim women and she suspects this narrow view of what a Muslim woman looks like is a prevalent one.

At 30 years of age, Samreena has long dark hair and striking features to match her South Asian heritage. She was raised in Sydney after her parents migrated from Bangladesh, home to more than 150 million people and the third most populous Muslim-majority country in the world.

Many of her female relatives in Bangladesh wear the hijab, but the opposite is true among Samreena's circle of family and friends in Australia. Her mother does not wear it, nor do many other older Bangladeshi women.

While many people are aware that Bangladesh is home to a large Muslim population, in Samreena's case, they often do not put the two together when it comes to her background.

Cultural misconception is of course not new and there are almost as many religious misconceptions. While the status of women in Muslim countries such as Saudi Arabia and Afghanistan is arguably a problem (though there is a possibility of change under a new, younger leader in Saudi Arabia at least) the position of women in Bangladesh is an example of how women are taking the lead in some Muslim societies. Bangladeshi women have made significant inroads since the country gained its independence in 1971—over the past 40 or so years, women have experienced increased political power, better jobs and improved education. Bangladesh reportedly has the highest proportion of educated women in the Islamic world. Since 2013, the Prime Minister of Bangladesh, its parliamentary Speaker and its Leader of the Opposition have all been women.

When Samreena's parents migrated to Australia when she was eight, the number of Australians with a Bangladeshi background was small. This remains so. About 53,000 Bangladeshis live in Australia, according to the 2012 census, and not all would identify as Muslim.

Samreena feels that her friendly personality contributes to misconceptions about her faith: 'There have been similar situations—especially in a work setting—where, because of how I behave, people have had no idea that I am a Muslim.'

It is as if people assume that Muslim women are very inhibited in their inter-personal dealings, which Samreena certainly isn't. She suspects this has something to do with the negative stories about Muslims in the media and that not enough people understand that, historically, Islam improved the status of women by granting them rights that were unprecedented for their times. Of course, the fact that these rights have not always translated into further improvement in the way some women are treated today in many Muslim countries (and beyond) raises questions about how Islam is being practised.

On hearing that Samreena prayed in one of the office meeting rooms, her colleague replied: 'So, you're practising then?'

Samreena: 'People often think, "Oh, she says she's a Muslim, but maybe she doesn't follow her religion." When I tell them about my praying and fasting—important pillars of Islam—they are very surprised.'

This is an issue that was brought into the public domain on the ABC's television program *Q&A* in 2016, when federal politician Pauline Hanson was shocked to learn that her then fellow politician and panellist, Sam Dastyari, was a Muslim. He is reportedly a non-practising one, which means that unlike Samreena he does not participate in the five daily prayer sessions or in fasting during Ramadan. Pauline Hanson's very public expression of surprise about what a Muslim looks like or how one behaves underlines a broader lack of understanding concerning diversity among Muslims, especially in terms of ethnicity and degree of religiosity.

Becoming a Muslim is relatively easy—one simply has to be prepared to recite the *Shahada*, the basic testimony of Islamic faith. However, it is difficult to put a figure on how many Muslims have *left* Islam, because it is an especially controversial topic, with views ranging from the belief that such a move is punishable by death to the notion that Islam promotes freedom of conscience.

Samreena's religion is known to her boss, an elderly man who has spent his life building a hugely successful family business that has a high public profile: 'He knows me as this Bangladeshi girl, and he can differentiate between what he sees on TV about Muslims and how I am as a person.'

Samreena says that her boss often stops by her desk when he is with guests and proudly announces: 'Do you know that this young lady is *Mos-lem*? The VIPs look at each other and say, "Oh really?"'

Samreena could interpret this whole scene as patronising, but she chooses not to be harsh about these things. She understands her boss is a product of his time, and in his mind, he is complimenting her.

'I just laugh, and say to the VIPs—"Whatever he says, he's right. He's the boss".'

Like Samreena, Elma has been the recipient of many a 'But-you-don't-look-like-a-Muslim' remark.

She understands why this might be some people's first reaction: she has fair skin, light-coloured hair and does not wear a hijab. Elma could add to this list that she doesn't regularly pray five a times a day, only knows by heart a few prayers from the Quran and has a casual approach to clothes (leggings and singlets are her staples, items that would generally not be considered modest attire for a Muslim). Nor does her name, which she has been told means 'apple' in Turkish, sound very Muslim.

'People never pick it, but I am a Muslim,' she says firmly.

Elma notes the irony that a beard on a man is now considered a fashion statement, even though being bearded has for centuries been the signature look of Arab men everywhere. Some of them are Muslim, and usually they are not seen in the same positive light as a hipster. For the male Muslim, a beard is more likely than not going to mark him out as 'a man of Middle Eastern appearance', which has become modern code for some extremely unflattering descriptions.

On more occasions than she would like, Elma has also been party to conversations where others have been caught out speaking of Muslims in a derogatory way without realising they are actually talking about her religion.

'One time, my friends' neighbour was complaining about some Muslim neighbours being noisy. When I told her I was a Muslim and that the noise those people were making had nothing to do with their religion—they were just noisy people—her jaw dropped.'

She continues: 'I don't like it when people say negative things about Muslims. I don't like getting into arguments, but why judge us all? The people saying such things usually don't read about Islam or look into it for themselves; then they meet Muslims like me and start to reconsider their views.'

Elma was born in Bosnia and has observed some differences between Arab Muslims and Muslims like herself from other ethnic or cultural backgrounds: 'We are more relaxed about religion, and a lot of people never pick we're Muslim.'

When Elma and her mother came to Australia as refugees in 1996, they left behind relatives in Bosnia who had either survived the civil war of the early 1990s or returned from another country at the end of it. Her mother lost both parents during the war: Elma says her family believes that her grandfather was burned in his home, while her grandmother disappeared, her body never found (she had wanted to stay in her home with her husband and refused to escape with Elma's mother). Her mother's three brothers and their sons—nine in total—were also killed in the war.

'When my mum sees footage of the Syrians fleeing their homes and trying to get to Europe, she says it reminds her of the time we arrived at the station in Vienna and didn't know anyone.' Elma was a one year old in her mother's arms at the time.

Now in her mid twenties, Elma is a regular visitor to Bosnia. Her cousins are much more conservative, especially the older generation, with the females donning the hijab. Elma's mother does not wear it, and has sometimes been looked down on by other Muslims, including in Australia, for not doing so.

Elma doesn't feel judged by her relatives overseas, although she admits she dresses more modestly when she visits. She is also convinced that if the war had not broken out she would still be living in Bosnia and probably be a far more religious person.

On a recent trip back, she noticed some big social changes. New groups were coming into Bosnia, leading to increased gentrification and driving up property prices, to the point that some locals were moving further away in search of cheaper housing. This, of course, is a story that is not unique to Bosnia, and Elma is aware of the debate going on in Australia about the impact of overseas buyers on the growing cost of real estate. However, Elma hopes that Bosnia, while trying to overcome its past divisions, can maintain its essence.

She herself has never forgotten her roots and is fluent in Bosnian. Elma is keen to pass on her knowledge to the younger generation of Australians with a Bosnian background, volunteering as a teacher at a Saturday language school.

Growing up as a teenager in Sydney, she has memories of attending community social events at the Bosnian Centre in Leppington. It is the site of annual war commemorations, sombre events, but at other times, it has been transformed into a concert hall for singers from Bosnia, invited to Australia to continue the social and cultural bonds between the two countries.

While all new migrants to Australia can face difficulties with resettlement, Elma notes that Bosnian Muslims who came after the war became Westernised more quickly than other groups. She puts this down to the idea that, 'Bosnia is part of Europe, so many Bosnians already have that outlook and are able to adapt more easily.'

If there is one message from both Samreena and Elma's experiences, it's that no two Muslims are the same. 'And not all Muslims look 'Muslim', whatever that means,' Samreena sighs.

It's worth noting that, in an era where the world is on high alert over terrorism, a distinctly Arab name can also create its own set of challenges—including for many Muslim men.

In early 2016, Karim, a civil engineer from Sydney, ordered a pair of Gucci sunglasses from a high-end online retailer in London. There seemed nothing exceptional about this, and yet the complications of this online shopping purchase were alarming.

The retailer had advertised that Karim's package would arrive in the mail within three working days. It didn't. Some days later, inquiries revealed that London's customs authority had held it. Inquiring about the delay, Karim received an email from the retailer: 'According to DHL, we were advised that your personal information is required for shipment held by the denied parties team.'

DHL, they reported, screens all parties to a shipment against restricted party lists maintained by the United Nations, the European Union and the United States government. Karim himself was identified as 'A valid match to a name on one of the lists, or; a probable match to a name on one of the lists.' If Karim required further information on 'trade sanctions and denied parties', the email advised, some 'helpful websites that explain the sanctions and embargoes imposed by the UN, EU and US Government are also provided.'

After further queries about his sunglasses, he was required to provide a copy of his passport by a certain time and date 'in order to prevent this shipment being abandoned and destroyed'. It turned out that Karim's name matched that of an individual on some type of watch list. He needed to prove that he was not the same person in order to have his sunglasses released.

It is hard not to argue for stricter security measures and checks given the current climate. Yet it should be noted that Muslims also contend with the myriad consequences of terrorism events as they go about their everyday lives.

Karim stuck it out for those Gucci glasses. They arrived, three weeks late and long after the excitement of the purchase had worn off. While he waited, Karim continued to receive invitations from the online shop to buy their latest offerings. 'Why, so that I wait weeks to get them?' he laughed.

11

Ever after

Nouha is not used to standing on the sidelines. As a 38-year-old school teacher, she is always ready to step in, take charge and direct her students.

So it wasn't easy to take a back seat at her mother Fatima's burial, shepherded—along with her sister and aunt—by an elderly male mourner into a spot behind the other men who stood encircling her mother's grave.

Earlier, the three women had been the ones to stand at her mother's bedside in the hospital. She was a pious woman, and although very ill, had still been aware of what was going on around her. As such, she needed no reminder or encouragement to recite verses from the Quran as the end was nearing. Muslims who still have their faculties would be keen for their last words to be a declaration of the *Shahada*.

Nouha had hoped for a happy ending to this cancer story, but it never came. The three women watched her mother take her last breath. Fatima had been there for three weeks; the cancer, four years.

Nouha remembers touching her mother's body as it was cold with death.

A short time after Fatima was pronounced dead, Nouha collected herself and walked outside the hospital to phone her sheikh. As a Muslim, her mother's body would need to be treated in a certain way and Nouha was anxious for his advice about what to do next. It struck her that it had been several years since her mother's diagnosis, yet she was so uninformed and ill-prepared about how to handle things from here on.

The sheikh was quick to respond; he organised for an Islamic association to transport Fatima's body to the mosque at Lakemba, a suburb in Sydney's south-west. In a specially-designed room at the site, her body would be prepared for burial in accordance with Islamic law. Nouha was informed that for a reasonable fee, the association provided all of the services for burial and funeral arrangements, including transport to its centre and the cemetery; washing of the body; and shrouding ahead of funeral prayers that could be held at the mosque.

When a Muslim dies, the doctrine is clear: they are to be pre-pared for burial as quickly as possible, ideally within 24 hours. This is because any delay for the purpose of mourning or viewing the corpse is forbidden, and this also ensures the body is kept in its natural state as much as possible as Muslims believe they are departing from this life to the afterlife. An autopsy is also to be resisted, unless formally required by the police or authorities. In the case of a deceased woman, the body is looked after by female staff, following strict guidelines.

This was the first time Nouha had experienced death up close.

'It was a big eye opener,' she recalls of the process. 'We didn't have much input.'

Fatima had passed away at 6.45 a.m., and by midday the same day, Nouha and all her Lebanese-Australian family were at the mosque. As the staff in the washroom took control of the situation, Nouha visited the female section of the prayer hall to recite Quranic verses. However, she was interrupted by an older woman who had known her mother and wanted to ask why Nouha wasn't downstairs attending to her mother's body. Nouha was surprised, unaware that family members could be involved in the washing of the deceased.

'I would have liked to have been informed that I could have been a part of it, as I didn't know that there was an expectation that her daughters would be involved,' Nouha explains.

On further reflection, however, she maintains she has no regrets about not being present. 'I knew from seeing my mother in a dead state at the hospital that humans look different when their heart is no longer pumping and for me personally, I didn't want to be any closer to that because my emotions were still very raw.

'Having spent the last few weeks of my mum's life with her in hospital, I don't think she would have wanted anyone to see her while she was being washed, including me.'

Nouha continued with her prayers, asking Allah to be merciful and forgiving to her mother. She knew that most people say this about the dead, but Fatima had been a loving and caring person and Nouha could not think of her having done anything in her life that was so bad that she would not be granted entry to Paradise (*Jannah*).

But Nouha also understood that Allah would be the judge of that, not her. When Muslims are young, they are fore-warned that when a person stands before Allah on the Day of Judgment, they will do so alone. No one will be there to inter-cede on their behalf for any personal failures or misdeeds. All Nouha could do was to pray that her mother's good deeds (*hasanat*) outweighed the bad.

As the eldest daughter, Nouha had taken the most interest in her parents' welfare over the years and had shouldered much of the burden of organising her mother's medical care as her illness took hold.

There was never any question that she would go to the cemetery for her own mother's burial, and not a single person in her family resisted the idea when that time came. However, growing up, Nouha had heard that some Muslim women were actively discouraged from attending burials.

'It's not accepted that women will be there because the thinking is that women get too emotional, and that's not what's needed at that time,' Nouha says of her understanding of the role of women at Islamic burials.

While Islam does not strictly forbid women from the cemetery during burials, they are strongly discouraged from attending and cautioned against dramatic public displays of grief. Wailing or shrieking is not permitted. The cultural attitude that women are less likely to control their grief at gravesites remains among some Muslims, which explains Nouha's interpretation.

Attending the burial was another first for her.

'When we arrived,' she explains, 'we walked towards the plot and there was an old man there—he was traffic control—and he directed us where to stand. It was away from the grave so that we didn't get too close to where the men were digging a hole in the ground.'

The women, who were unable to get an uninterrupted view of the proceedings due to the large number of male mourners who had gathered, stood about ten metres back.

While Nouha, her sister and aunt could express their grief through tears, they tried hard to keep their emotions in check by focusing on their prayers for Fatima.

Muslims are taught from a young age to understand that death is a natural part of life, and God decides when that life is taken away. So questioning why the deceased had to die is seen as questioning the will of Allah. For them, death is not the end, as a human is shifting from one state to another, and on the Day of Judgment, Allah will decide on their next path—heaven or hell (and how long the stint in the latter will be) depending on one's deeds on Earth.

'I wasn't surprised about where we were asked to stand because I have always known that, culturally, that's the way it's done,' Nouha says. 'I was already emotional and I knew that if I had gotten any closer, I would have lost it. I would not have been able to control myself.'

Special Quranic verses are recited by the sheikh at the grave. Muslims do this first and foremost for their own spiritual nourishment, hoping that these words will have some impact for the deceased.

An image from that day that Nouha says she will never forget is of her older brother digging their mother's grave.

'He was standing inside the hole; it was so deep all I could see was his head and it actually brought me comfort knowing that he had taken control of the process.'

She continues: 'He helped to lift my mother's body out of a simple casket. She was wrapped in a plain white cloth and lowered into the grave. Earth was then shovelled over her body.'

Muslims are not buried in a casket unless this is to be done for legal or public health reasons.

Nouha found the pace of a Muslim burial to be a mercy: 'Mum died in the morning and by 2 p.m. the same day, every-thing was done and dusted.'

But it was just the beginning of the mourning process for Nouha and her family. For the next three days, the sheikh visited their home to recite Quranic verses and lead prayers for the mourners. A crowd of mourners developed daily at her parents' suburban home. While the formal mourning period usually lasts for three days, Nouha and her family will personally mourn for much longer.

The family had much work to do in hosting these mourners, including all of the women who had been unable to make it to the mosque or attend the burial. They had many helpers—relatives and friends—who jumped in to assist with the non-stop serving of refreshments. Dates are a popular snack to offer mourners, as it was what the Prophet Muhammad ate when he broke his fast during Ramadan.

Nouha's school colleagues had supported her through the most difficult days of her mother's illness, taking turns to check in with her and to cook and deliver meals.

One of the teachers, Mary, who had known Nouha for five years, had taken an interest in Islamic rituals. Mary had a Greek background and could relate to Nouha's experience of being raised in a migrant family with a strong culture. So when the teachers at the school suggested they send flowers to Nouha after hearing about Fatima's death, Mary stepped in and explained that Muslims bury their dead quickly and without any fanfare, including decorations such as flowers. And unlike the traditions of other cultures that focus on celebrating the life of the dead with paraphernalia and music, Muslims are firmly opposed to a colourful approach to death or mourning.

Mary knew that Nouha would have appreciated a condolence gesture such as flowers. However, with her knowledge about Muslim life, she suggested to her fellow teachers that they leave a mark that was both respectful of the Muslim experience and would have a longer lifespan than the proposed flowers. She would buy four small garden plants for Nouha and her family, and would suggest that two could be planted at the grave.

Knowing what she does now about how the Muslim community handles death, Nouha doesn't think that she would have done anything differently. But she also thinks about the impact of the approach to burials on her female friends.

While someone like Mary would have been discouraged from attending, the presence of her non-Muslim male colleagues, for instance, would not have been controversial, as they would have been able to blend in at the cemetery simply on the basis of their gender. This is not an easy thing to explain to non-Muslims without accusations of gender discrimination. Nouha is thankful it is not something she had to worry about since everything happened so fast on the day her mother died.

The day after the burial, Nouha rose early to attend her mother's grave and recite verses from the Quran. She hadn't been able to get close to it the day before because of the long queue of male mourners that had gathered to pay their respects to her father and brothers near the fresh grave.

A small, simple plaque had been erected at the cemetery to identify her mother. Strictly speaking, even this is considered out of line with Islamic teachings regarding spartan burial sites. However, as the number of Muslims has grown, it is expected in modern times that the place of a dead Muslim will be marked out. Nouha and her siblings decided to go one step further and invest in a marble headstone. This was not about her family being flashy; they simply wanted something that would both appropriately honour their mother and withstand the elements over time.

Nouha later ensured that the plants from her fellow teachers were dug into the soil near the grave. As they grow, she says, they serve as an important reminder that life goes on.

'I had seen my mum go through pain for four years. I think the way things were finally handled at the burial was simple and respectful.'

Some Muslim women find it hard to accept the cultural position on female attendance at burials. Kadija's story—told second-hand—is one such example.

For her, the blunt message that she could not attend her grandfather Samir's funeral felt almost violent—the very opposite of the happy memories she had of growing up with him.

Samir had lived a long life with her grandmother, Mariam. They migrated to Australia from Lebanon as newlyweds and were married for over fifty years. When he died, Mariam's only wish was to attend his burial. Kadija felt strongly supportive of her grandmother's position and took it upon herself to explain to everyone that her grandmother's presence was not a religious protest. She simply wanted to be present. It was not lost on Kadija that the strongest opposition to their attendance came from men who hardly knew her grandfather. They were not regular visitors to his home and it seemed cruel to her that those who didn't know him well were now trying to organise his life in death.

After some heated conversations, everybody finally understood that Kadija and her grandmother would be at the burial.

On the day, a simple, plastic white chair was placed on one side of the grave for her grandmother. She needed it not only due to her age; all the emotions she had experienced since her husband's death had made her even more fragile.

Then there is Suhar—another Lebanese-Australian woman. Due to serious health complications, her baby daughter unfortunately never left the Sydney hospital where she had been born five months earlier.

Suhar's relative, Wafa, witnessed first-hand the family drama that ensued over the burial.

While she waited in a hospital room for her daughter's body to be formally released to the family, Suhar brought up the subject of attending the burial. Wafa listened closely as Suhar's mother-in-law gently explained to Suhar that it was recommended that women not be present.

Suhar, her emotions understandably raw, dismissed her mother-in-law's intervention: 'No, I want to go. This is my daughter . . . I want to go.'

Her mother-in-law then sympathetically withdrew from the conversation, not wanting to add to Suhar's distress. Not that this brought a resolution in Suhar's favour.

Her father, Tarek, who was also present, stepped in with more forceful language to explain the cultural position on women at burials to his daughter. As Suhar attempted to dig in, his tone became even more firm: 'It's *haram*.'

An anguished Suhar continued to appeal to him but her father was unmoved. His understanding of religion trumped his daughter's feelings because as he saw it, he was not speaking from emotion. All those present heard the air of finality in his voice when he replied: 'No.' Suhar was stunned by her father's words, but stopped fighting him.

Although sad for Suhar, Wafa does not regret that she did not step in to help her to challenge her father since she did not equate his hardline approach with coldness. Her reasons for this are simple: 'If you've got a senior man who knows more about our religion telling you not to go, what are you going to do, go against him? Sometimes you just have to do what is being asked. He knows better.' Other Muslim fathers in his position would have done the same, she maintains.

When the baby's body was transported to the mosque's washroom, she was delicately wrapped in a hospital blanket, her tiny body on a stretcher that was placed at a basin wide and long enough for an adult's body.

Wafa and a couple of other witnesses were allowed to look on with Suhar as an older woman carefully undressed the baby. She slowly soaped and rinsed the body while softly reciting words from the Quran. Powder was also diluted into the water to scent the body, before it was dried with a towel.

Several pieces of white cotton cloth were then cut to size, the material expertly handled as it was pulled off a roll attached to a wall like those seen at a haberdashery. First the body was wrapped, with another piece placed over the head and tied at the neck like a headscarf. At this point, the face was still showing so that family members including the baby's father (who by now had entered the room) could say their goodbyes. The baby's precious face was then covered with a cloth, while the rest of her body was wrapped with ribbons tied at both ends to keep all of the material in place. In the final act of preparation for burial, a small rug with Islamic verses was placed atop the little wooden coffin after it was sealed.

Given its size, the baby's father, accompanied by other male relatives for moral support, picked up the box on his own for the short walk to the mosque, where male mourners were waiting to conduct special prayers ahead of the burial at the cemetery. The women held their prayers in a separate quarter.

Muslim parents are likely to take comfort in the knowledge that, as most Islamic scholars maintain, babies go straight to Paradise since they have no deeds to be judged by God.

With the burial process for Muslims, there is surely one thing firmly in its favour, as Nouha had earlier identified. The whole affair is conducted without fanfare or commercialisation. No White Ladies need be present at such funerals, because Islam demands a stripped-back burial in every way. For many families, the simplicity is a relief.

12

Headstrong

When Mehal arrives at a train station, she does not study the indicator board for what time her train will arrive. She is too busy scanning the platform for a wall to stand against, which has become part of a routine personal risk assessment she undertakes every time she catches a train.

By positioning herself against a wall, Mehal strategises that there is less chance she will be caught off-guard. Her fear stems from a report in November 2015 of a man who appeared to push a woman wearing a hijab into an oncoming train on London's Underground. While follow-up details about the motive for the reported attack were sketchy, that the victim was wearing a hijab was enough to force Mehal, who also wears one, to consider how to better protect herself while out in public.

As she is visibly identifiable as a Muslim, Mehal, aged 30 and with Lebanese heritage, has trained herself to think: 'How can I put enough room between myself and a would-be attacker?'

And if past personal experience is anything to go by, Mehal has every reason to be taking such precautions.

'How would you like it if I chopped off your head?'

These are the words with which Mehal was threatened three years ago as she stood in line to withdraw money from an ATM at a suburban shopping strip in Sydney. Asked to describe the perpetrator, she states: 'An old Anglo woman.'

Another woman standing in line behind Mehal tried to distract Mehal from the abuse by making small talk. Mehal now thinks this bystander's actions were about building allegiance, which meant that neither had to engage with the abusive woman.

Mehal did not stick around to confront her abuser. She quickly withdrew her money and drove to a scheduled acupuncture appointment that day. A PhD student at the time, Mehal had much to contend with and found that acupuncture relieved her stress. She made her appointment on time that day and never mentioned a word about the abuse to the practitioner.

It was only later that day, in the safety of her home, that Mehal was hit with the emotional fallout of what had occurred earlier at the ATM. She was shocked by the encounter.

Mehal took to Facebook to inform her online friends of the abuse to which she had been subjected. Her post read: 'Nothing like some good ol' fashioned racism, in Revesby. No, I wouldn't like my head chopped off, but thank you kindly for the inquiry.'

Mehal was inundated with responses from friends and acquaintances urging her to report the matter to the police, a move she had not considered, despite being a trained sociologist whose work relied heavily on the collection and interpretation of statistics.

She took their advice, but was left disappointed by the police response. 'They basically said they couldn't do anything about it because it had already happened, and to call them next time while it's actually happening.'

Mehal strongly disagrees with the police officer's approach, since she did not feel safe enough to take any action at the time.

When one of her friends who has had some experience dealing with the police asked if she had been given a report number by the officer, Mehal informed her that she was given no such record. Her friend explained that this likely meant her complaint—which she believes was an attack on Mehal based on her religion—was never officially recorded.

Individuals who have experienced major trauma or distress often regret not responding in a certain way during an incident. Not Mehal. 'I wouldn't change how I reacted. My nature is to placate or get out of the situation.'

But she does regret that the encounter shattered her sense of safety in that neighbourhood—she had been a frequent visitor to the shopping area since she was little girl, as it was not far from her home and she grew up thinking of it as her local hangout.

'That was my community; it's where my childhood friends lived. But I started to think . . . it's just like everywhere else.'

Everyone in her circle seemed to have an opinion about how they would have handled the matter. One of her friends revealed that she had taken the opposite posture to Mehal: when she was verbally abused by a stranger because of her hijab, she chased the man away.

But Mehal was unmoved, insisting that her small frame also potentially made her more physically vulnerable. 'That was her natural gut reaction, to chase the man. But if, like me, you are not used to taking someone on, now is not the time to do it.'

Perhaps a more intimidating experience than the ATM incident occurred some years earlier, when a carload of men yelled for her to 'Go home' as she walked to the shops during her lunch break.

'It was scary. Even though there were other people around, nobody did anything. I ended up just walking away. If they had stopped and got out of the car, I don't know what I would have done.'

When she returned to her office, Mehal confided in one of her female colleagues about what had happened. She was supportive, asked Mehal if she needed anything and offered some self-defence tips, which have stayed with Mehal.

'She told me to consider what I had on me that I could use as weapon. Apparently my hijab pins would be good.' Mehal had never thought of this, and found the idea quite innovative.

The most personally offensive incident occurred while Mehal was on her way to catch a train via a busy pedestrian tunnel. She had just lodged a major university assignment and was on a high as she hurriedly made her way to Central station in Sydney. Speaking on her mobile phone to a friend, Mehal noticed a man walking past her in the opposite direction.

Before she had time to think, she looked down to find saliva dripping off one side of her sneaker. She continued to walk fast, rifling through her handbag for a tissue to remove the fluid. Mehal never looked back, but heard two women behind her say of the man's actions: 'That is so disgusting.'

Mehal puts her decision not to engage with the man down to being in a rush and not having time to process what happened. But she is clear about what she thinks was his main intention: 'He wanted to humiliate me.'

Mehal again turned to Facebook to share information about the 'random freak' who had just spat on her: 'I just got spat on . . . Nothing cures OCD [obsessive compulsive disorder] like a 40-minute train trip covered in the remnants of somebody else's saliva. Humans suck.'

While others may not have been as calm as Mehal if they had been subjected to such a vile act, Mehal insists: 'When you deal with these things every day, it's the smallest things that actually get under your skin. The bigger things, they're easier to compartmentalise. I don't want to be preoccupied with these things. I have places to go, deadlines to meet and friends to see. I don't want to spend my life in confrontation.'

But she is also keen not to underplay that the fear of being either verbally or physically attacked, or both, for being a Muslim is very real. For instance, she doubts she was the only Muslim woman in Australia who questioned whether she should go to work on the day in May 2017 that news broke of a suicide bombing aimed at concertgoers in the British city of Manchester.

Most people check their news feeds in the morning for the weather report or traffic update. Mehal only looks at hers if she has received a specific link from a friend, as it usually means that a terrorism-related incident has occurred somewhere in the world and it could have an impact on how she organises her day.

'After anything happens that's related to terrorism, I'm conscious of going out. I ask myself: "Do I need to go out today; maybe I should work from home today?"'

She usually forces herself to go about her normal business. 'Nothing good will come of staying home.'

On the day of the concert bombing, she took so long to make a decision about whether to catch the train to work that she ended up being late. She had spent the morning mulling things over with her husband, who urged her to go to work as normal.

'This has a real effect on our lives, but in the end I decided I didn't want to restrict my movement.'

Mehal considers herself an informed person, and finds it hard to rationalise that she would consider locking herself away. 'I am not a weak person and people don't think of me in that way. But it's an internal battle that lots of Muslim women experience.'

Anecdotally, Muslim women bear the brunt of anti-Muslim sentiment on public transport and when shopping. More generally, reports of racism on public transport in Australia are increasingly making headlines, with those who look noticeably different or dare speak a foreign language in public also the targets of abuse. Such incidents are being captured on mobile devices and uploaded for public consumption to a wide audience.

Mehal counts herself lucky that she has so far had only safe journeys on the trains. Indeed, the most frustrating thing has been when commuters recognise that she is a Muslim from her hijab and try to engage her in conversation about politics. 'The train is my time to tune out, and catch up on things like podcasts. Believe it or not, Muslim women don't live their lives talking about just Islam and politics.'

Other Muslim women have not been so lucky on the trains. In December 2014, as a gunman held people hostage in a Sydney cafe, a train commuter reportedly posted on Facebook that she had witnessed a woman removing her hijab on the train. Her post prompted a Twitter user to start the hashtag 'illridewithyou'. Thousands of individuals then joined the campaign, offering to meet Muslims at their local train stations and to ride with them on their journey.

A couple of years before this campaign, Widyan, of an Iraqi background and then in her late teens, experienced a particularly ugly encounter on the train. Her memory of this was triggered by a report that Australian television journalist Jeremy Fernandez had been the victim of a racial attack on a Sydney bus. Fernandez tweeted at the time that he was called a 'black c*nt' and told to 'go back to my country' in front of his two-year-old daughter. Speaking later on ABC radio, the shaken journalist said the attack was about 'hate'.

'This wasn't about race, it was about hate . . . it happens every day in Australia, this is not a rare incident.'

His words resonated with Widyan, who wears a hijab and subsequently wrote online about her unpleasant experience on a Sydney train. She had boarded an overcrowded train home and gripped one of the handrails. Later in her journey, she spotted an empty seat and made her way to it, but before she had the chance to sit down, she was pushed aside by a burly man who looked like he had just walked off a worksite.

'Sorry love, I don't f*cking stand for anyone,' he snarled.

At this, Widyan retorted: 'That's fine, you can have the seat because you're older, but your attitude is disgusting.'

Caught off-guard by her comments, the man studied her and then spat: 'Look at you. You bought your camels here. I pay my taxes—I have a right to sit down on the train.'

Furious, Widyan replied: 'Everyone pays their taxes and everyone has paid for a ticket and we all have a right to sit down but clearly not everyone can. By the way, I'm an Australian so don't you dare give me that nonsense.'

But the man carried on: 'This is my country, born and bred, and I work hard and deserve to be here.'

A fed up Widyan finally fired back: 'No, this country is not "yours" . . . Look around you, look at the diversity in this carriage alone!'

The carriage then erupted with applause. Widyan remembers someone grabbing her hand with approval, but she was too caught up in the moment to notice who it was. Another woman rubbed her shoulder: 'Well done, love. You showed him what you're made of.'

Despite the support, the episode left Widyan shaking with fear and anger. 'It was only when I got off at my stop that I started to fully comprehend what had just happened.'

Like Widyan, Mehal is getting on with her life and has a message for those who seek to attack her because of her head covering: 'I am not going to spend my time educating you about the hijab or Islam, because I have things to achieve.'

Plenty of assumptions prevail about the hijab, including that Muslim women only wear it for religious reasons. Many, however, speak of wearing it for other reasons too, such as it is the typical thing to do in the country where they were born. Some women wear it for certain occasions only, like during a period of mourning to show their respect. Others may have been pressured to wear it.

For most women who wear the hijab, it is expected that it will be a life-long, permanent decision. Once on, it is considered very difficult to turn back from it. Those who change their mind can face harsh criticism, with questions raised about their commitment to Islam. In some circles, it is considered better to be a Muslim who has not yet made the decision to put on a hijab than to be one who has done so and then taken it off.

In some Western countries, women have been prompted to remove it to reduce the possibility that they will experience discrimination, for example, since the September 11 terrorist attacks and as the level of negative news about Muslims has become more intense. Then there are those who have taken the opposite stance, putting it on for the first time to show their support for their faith. Again, this is a demonstration of the different motivations at play with the hijab.

Just as the hijab is not a fixed marker, so too is the way it is worn. Like any garment or accessory, it comes in different shapes, sizes and colours, though the type most commonly worn in Western societies is the version that covers the head and neck (and leaves the face clear).

Global fashion houses have cottoned on to the market in catering to Muslim women who require modest clothing, some of whom reside in the most cashed-up societies in the world and are fashion conscious with a desire for luxury goods. In a climate where companies are increasingly competing for the fashion dollar, the clothing needs of this group of women has become the focus of some collections. Take Dolce & Gabbana, which in 2016 produced a collection of hijabs and *abayas* for Muslim customers in the Middle East.

A turban has also become a fashion accessory for Muslims and non-Muslims alike. Among some Muslims, a 'turbanista' is a term used to describe 'fashionistas who rock a turban'. However, the look has been criticised as *haram* by some Muslims.

Abyan knows something about the assumptions people make about a *hijabi*, the name given to Muslim women who don the hijab. Every day since she was thirteen, Abyan's morning ritual has involved choosing a scarf to match her outfit, be it her school uniform, clothes for work or a social occasion.

She comes from a Somali background and has found that people tend to be surprised to learn that Muslims can wear the head veil for a variety of reasons, and so, like any other major life decision, these motivations may change over time as an individual's life takes shape.

As a girl, Abyan says she attended *dugsi*, or Saturday language school in Somali, where she was taught about the Quran and to read and write in Arabic. She perceived that wearing the hijab was another step in her journey as a Muslim. 'I thought it was an act of worship and to safeguard my modesty.'

Abyan moved to Australia with her family when she was five. She started to wear the hijab when she reached Year 7 because that was what was expected—she was going through puberty and her older sisters had also worn it at that age. 'I chose to do it; I did see it as part of my identity,' Abyan explains. 'It was about belonging. My mum, sisters and elders wore it.'

The transition from primary to high school is a big moment in any young person's life, as is buying a school uniform for 'big' school. As part of this process, Abyan started to think about what a hijab would look like with her uniform. She wanted something to match her new school colours and decided on a navy-blue scarf, which she wore pinned at her chin and draped down her chest.

'I didn't ask anyone for help; I assumed that's how it was supposed to be worn.'

When she started to become self-conscious about her body in high school—a challenge experienced by many teenagers— Abyan began to feel some personal conflict about the hijab. At the time, she was also being targeted in the playground by other students, and called derogatory names such as 'Osama bin Laden'.

'The idea of removing it at school altogether never occurred to me. But I did start to wear it more fashionably; I would switch it up, and felt that by wearing it in different ways, I could be express myself.'

She also explains that the idea that it is worn permanently or full-time is not necessarily true for all Muslims, as some women wear it only for certain occasions. However, in Abyan's experience, some Muslims find it hard to accept this more casual position, or that other Muslims might wear anything other than a hijab to cover their hair. Somalis, for instance, sometimes wear hijabs styled as headwraps, and this is a part of their culture regardless of it being a hijab or not.

The Somali headwrap-look is something Abyan has experimented with, but has found that it too can invite questions about piety, with queries that range from, 'Are you really scarved?' to 'Are you a Muslim?'

Abyan maintains: 'We [those from Somali backgrounds] have particular ways of wearing the headwrap.'

***

While the angst Abyan felt about the hijab as a teenager has passed, recently her feelings about wearing it have changed. 'When you think about it, it is something you have to recommit to every day by putting it on.'

Now 28 and living and working in Sydney, Abyan woke up one morning and decided not to wear her hijab to work. A few days before, she had spent most of the day in a hair salon having her long, thick black hair braided for a female-only party.

When she had to dress for work the following day, she found it difficult to tuck her new long braids into her hijab. So she decided to leave her hair (a look which paid homage to her African heritage) out in public. She knew there was a touch of vanity about her thinking—she had spent a lot of time and money on her hair—but Abyan had enjoyed so much having her hair out at the party that she began to wonder whether she wanted to prolong that feeling.

'I don't know if I would have taken my hijab off if I didn't get my hair done that day. I don't know what came first.'

Many Muslim women, once they have made the decision to put on a hijab, speak of feeling naked without it in public. Abyan had no such qualms: 'I honestly didn't give it much thought.'

Her sentiment may surprise some people given how long she had been wearing it.

While Abyan feels excited to express a new part of herself, this experience is tinged with some trepidation about what others might think. She remains adamant, however, that whether she wears the hijab or not is her decision alone, and she does not have to seek permission from anyone about her plans.

That includes her family, who live in Adelaide.

Abyan concedes that her mother, whom she is yet to see in person since taking off her hijab, would not be happy about her decision. 'I know my mum would be disappointed. I would cop a lecture about the importance of hijab and to not forget my values.'

For now, she has confided in her older sisters, who have given her the emotional space she needs to explore her feelings and advised her to be herself.

Could living in Sydney be Abyan's way of hiding from her mother's expected disapproval? While she wouldn't be the first person to move away from home so that she could do her own thing, Abyan insists that had she been living in Adelaide, she would have still found a way to keep it from her mother until she was confident of what she wanted to do, and 'then put up with whatever happens'.

Somali-born Australians are among this country's newer migrant groups, with many arriving in the early 1990s as refugees from Somalia's civil war. Somalia is made up of mostly Sunni Muslims, and traditionally women will wear a headwrap called a *shash*. Religion features in many aspects of life, with children encouraged to be familiar with the Quran before they start school.

Many Somali-Australians have set up home in the Sydney suburb of Auburn. When Abyan visits the area, as she does regularly, her attire always includes her hijab because she knows she will inevitably run into a relative or friend, and she does not want to invite judgment or questions. 'It's enough that as a female I wear pants, which is seen as improper,' Abyan adds.

The expectation that women will wear a long skirt or loose dress is an attitude that prevails among some of the older and more conservative men and women who have come to Australia from Somalia.

However, it is a different story for her in the neighbouring suburb of Lidcombe, only one train stop away. When she meets up with an acquaintance there, Abyan does so without her hijab as she does not expect to bump into someone from her community.

Abyan denies that she feels like one person in Auburn and another in Lidcombe. 'It's about self-preservation. If I were to walk around Auburn without the hijab, I would feel anxiety about attracting attention; I just don't want awkward encounters.'

So Abyan does what many people grappling with an element of their identity do—she compartmentalises, and shifts and adapts between locations where she knows people and those where she doesn't.

Yet her decision to drop the hijab has not gone unnoticed by her friends. When one girlfriend viewed a photo on Snapchat of Abyan out without her hijab, she wrote: 'I didn't know you were a half-jabi girl. Tell me more about this? [Smiley face]'.

'Half-jabi' was not a term Abyan had heard before. (An online search reveals a 'shoutout' tweet from one woman to 'hijabis, no-jabis, glamjabis, half-jabis and all Muslim girls'.)

Abyan texted her friend back: 'He he he, I just go with the flow, I don't make a habit of it.'

The next time Abyan met her friend in person, they talked about the hijab and her friend confided that she too has thought of taking it off.

Abyan has considered whether her recent fluidity with the hijab is an act of rebellion many girls get out of their system in their teens, and she is just catching up, although she sees it more as a general experimentation with her appearance.

Abyan is keen to explain that just because she has taken off the hijab for the time being does not mean she is questioning her faith or wavering in her commitment to it. While her feelings may have recently changed about the hijab, this has not altered the modest way in which she dresses—loose pants with a long shirt that sits over her hips is her go-to dress code. 'I haven't bared anything,' she observes. 'I still act the same way; I am still committed to my faith and the modesty is in my behaviour.'

Nevertheless, she has identified that as she goes about her days without the hijab, it has become evident, as she puts it, that she has one less thing to worry about: 'I am not visibly Muslim.'

As she tries to navigate how people—those who already know her and those who don't—perceive her without the hijab, Abyan has had to deal with her manager asking her if anything is wrong, while her colleagues have complimented her on her braids. And she has noticed a difference in how people treat her. Muslims speak of a sisterhood and brother-hood, and it is common for them to respectfully acknowledge each other in public with the Arabic words, '*Assalamu alaikum*' ('Peace be with you'), if they recognise someone as a Muslim even when they are complete strangers.

During a recent trip to the post office, Abyan was served by a woman in a hijab and expected to hear this traditional greeting; when she didn't, she had to remind herself that she was not wearing a hijab.

How would she know I'm a Muslim? Abyan asked herself.

While she is not currently visibly identifiable as a Muslim, there is one thing that Abyan cannot change: 'The colour of my skin.'

When she was in primary school, she recalls that no one else looked like her.

She has also experienced surprise from some Australians that Muslims can be 'black', raising questions about how Muslims are represented in public discourse.

'It is a local issue because most people's perception in Australia—even among some Muslims—of a Muslim is not black or African, so we don't feel part of the community. Sometimes I don't feel like I am reflected.'

Abyan has also become more concerned about what she describes as 'anti-black sentiment'. She thinks that personal safety is a growing problem for Muslim women in a hijab. In particular, she expresses her deep shock at the murder of an American Muslim teenager in June 2017 as she walked home from a mosque near Washington, with the possibility that it was an anti-Muslim hate crime an angle under investigation: 'That shook me to my core. I thought about my young nieces walking to school in Adelaide and whether they would be the victims of random violence. It weighs on your mind; it did make me scared to be wearing the hijab.'

Abyan also grapples with the contradiction she feels about a key purpose for the hijab—to draw less attention to a woman—and cannot help but wonder whether in a secular country like Australia it works the opposite way.

Another pressure a woman in a hijab can feel is the responsibility to represent Islam, whether they want to or not.

'Sometimes questions come from a place of curiosity and that's fine, but sometimes it does feel like an interrogation and that you are only qualified to speak about things that are about Islam. You can't just be a person who enjoys something and be a Muslim; you are always a Muslim first.'

Speaking of the public nature of being a *hijabi*, Abyan explains that sometimes on a crowded train, she might lose her cool. Often she has to watch her behaviour to avoid the impression among other passengers that Muslims are rude as she does not want assumptions to be made that Muslims are pushy, or to make Islam look bad.

'And that's exhausting . . . to filter yourself and always see yourself through that filter of other people all day long.'

Abyan concedes that some days she is unapologetic about what she has to do—hijab or no hijab—to navigate her way in and out of a busy train, which can require an angelic amount of patience.

Abyan did not plan to be in the position in which she now finds herself. She is convinced that she is going through a phase, and volunteers that she will go back to wearing the hijab full-time. 'It's not permanent.'

Perhaps these feelings also explain why she does not see removing it for the time being as a life-changing experience, again emphasising: 'It's not a lasting decision.'

Later, though, after giving things more thought, Abyan reveals that she is actually undecided about putting it back on full time.

One thing she is adamant about, however, is that her respect for the hijab has not diminished, nor the important religious significance it holds for her.

'I have worn it all my life, but right now, I don't feel like I am betraying myself by not wearing it.'

13

Keeping score

'What's this thing you do every weekend?' Amna's father, Bassam, would ask every Saturday.

Somehow Amna always found a way of responding without really telling him what was going on. She got away with this approach for a while, but eventually Amna had to explain the real reason she wasn't around much anymore on the weekends: she was putting together a girls' AFL team.

'End it! Let it go!' was her father's swift response in Arabic, saying it like he was shooing away a fly.

'I can't . . . I have twenty girls who love playing football,' Amna appealed to him.

Her father's behaviour reminded her of the emotional blackmail she had experienced from him growing up. 'Don't you want me to be happy?' was always his response whenever

Amna got involved in something he didn't approve of. To her father, from a Lebanese Muslim background, life would be simple if only she would abide by his wishes.

'Yes,' Amna had always replied, 'I want you to be happy . . . But I want to be happy too.'

This is a line that many children have delivered to their parents at some point in their lives, but for Amna, the dispute was about an activity that would not raise an eyebrow in most other Australian households. For many young people, weekend sport is ritual, with parents crisscrossing the city to ferry their children to parks in far-flung suburbs.

Amna worried that playing sport would make her father think of her as less of a woman, Arab or Muslim. So to keep up with his expectations of what a female should be like at home, she made sure that she stayed on top of her chores.

'I was trying to be the kind of woman that he thinks is the right kind of woman,' Amna says of her relationship with her father.

From a young age, Amna was acutely aware that being a girl meant she was different when it came to playing sports.

Every weekend it was a family tradition to meet with relatives and friends for a picnic at a local park. A barbecue would be fired up and plates of homemade tabouli and hummus lined a long wooden table that had been secured early in the morning by one of the picnickers.

Amna noticed that at the start of every gathering all the young boys and girls would muck around together with a football. Then, when the game started to get more physical, she and the other girls would be asked to leave the field so that the boys could continue with *their* game. Amna found it hard to shake the unfairness she felt every time this happened. It became obvious that being a girl meant that the boys thought she wasn't up to the challenge of playing sport with them.

Recruiting Australian Muslim girls from a Lebanese background to a sporting team was a big challenge in itself. Doing it with Muslim girls from other ethnicities was an even bigger one, Amna found. The reasons young women usually gave her for not wanting to play ranged from 'My dad said no' to 'My brother doesn't like it' to 'I'm getting married soon, so what's the point?'

Amna found that Bosnian-Australians seemed the most open to the idea, but those from a Somali background were a whole different ballgame—and proved to be the most difficult to crack. 'Mate, give up, we are not there yet as a community,' she was told by one Somali-Australian woman.

Various opinions are held on the role of Muslim women participating in sport. In some Muslim countries, women face a total ban. In Australia, the resistance comes not from a lack of opportunities in the public sphere but from attitudes among

Muslims themselves. Some believe that a woman moving her body by running, jumping or kicking in front of men puts her modesty at risk. The uniform is also a concern.

Amna laughs off the notion that kicking a football exposes a woman's body in an inappropriate way. She is sufficiently in tune with community attitudes, though, to understand that the idea of a Muslim woman playing sports—especially in a serious or professional capacity—is often perceived as radical.

An online search uncovers a fair amount of research around the world about the lack of participation by Muslim women in sports and physical education, both on a personal level and competitively or professionally. For all the formal reasons put forward, however, it sometimes takes an amateur voice to provide insights that are hard to come by anywhere else.

What follows is a list posted on a blog called Happy Muslim Mama ('Muslim Women and Sports Participation', 13 May 2011) of one Muslim woman's thoughts on the possible reasons for the predicament Muslim women find themselves in when it comes to playing sport. While they may not be universal, the author points out that these issues have often been missed by educators, researchers and parents, because individuals prefer not to talk about them openly.

1. A bad experience of physical education (PE) in school. Sometimes teachers do not understand individual needs and are unwilling to be flexible.

2. Dress code. Muslim girls are raised to cover their arms and legs for modesty, so wearing a swimming costume or PE uniform is often a no-no.

3. Body hair. Some teenage girls develop a layer of dark, visible hair before they know about shaving or waxing, so exposing their arms and legs can be embarrassing.
4. Periods. Muslim girls prefer not to use tampons. Therefore, sports like swimming are not possible during this time of the month.
5. Mixed-gender lessons. Many Muslim women feel much more comfortable in a women-only environment.
6. Lack of parental support. Some think that if sport is not going to help their daughter's education, then what's the point, especially if one has to be away from home at night.
7. Timing of practice. Many lessons happen at night and some parents don't like their daughters staying out.

More institutions, such as Australian schools, are looking at ways to respond to diversity, for example by allowing the hijab and modest dress for PE within safety requirements.

Amna argues that such physical activity is in line with Islam's stance on health. For example, many Muslims point to a *Hadith* (reported sayings of the Prophet Muhammad) that describes the Prophet racing in the desert with his wife Ayesha to demonstrate that women should be involved in exercise/sport in public.

Amna is convinced that her decision to take the lead in this area has had an unforeseen impact on how she is viewed by men. She is 28 and single; she knows many men but only as friends. Amna maintains that this is because 'at the end of the day, they are not married to me.' So they are men who can accept her forthrightness on the sports field, though not anywhere else, she feels.

Amna is not overly concerned about this because she came to the conclusion at a young age that she was unlikely to marry a man with the same Muslim Lebanese background. 'Did I think I was going to find a man in my community? Absolutely not,' Amna says. She was so adamant about it that she forewarned her mother. Convert, white, non-Arab: that's how she described her future husband to her. 'I said, "Let me tell you, I am not going to marry a Lebo guy. I am going to marry a white boy who is a convert."'

Her mother's shock was not unexpected: 'How is your dad going to communicate with him?' This is a common concern among parents whose first language is not English. 'English is the common language in Australia,' Amna replied casually. 'He will be fine.'

Amna finds non-Arab men are less judgmental of her. 'There's something about how patriarchy plays out in Arab communities. Many women feel disempowered, because of their religion and culture, in a way that's not happening in the wider community.'

She agrees there are gender issues in that wider world too, but for Amna, life seems much easier and fairer in that space.

'I am single because of my ideas about relationships and about men in the Muslim Lebanese-Australian community. The men who would accept me for who I am—independent, someone with a strong sense of self—they are few and far between.'

Amna has a theory that male converts to Islam are more open and supportive about a women's role in the community, and that this is confirmed by the experience of one of her fellow AFL team members who has a strong personality, a successful career and plays sport. Her husband is a convert and comes to her games every weekend—a picture of support Amna is yet to personally experience.

'She found someone compatible, who embraces her strengths.'

When challenged, Amna admits that a recent experience has got her rethinking her theory about converts. She was attracted to Joe—a participant at a workshop where she held a presentation about the relationship between health issues and women's participation in sport. He was 30, a convert and divorced. Joe actively pursued her; Amna says she was keen on him especially since he was understanding of her busy schedule.

Amna thinks Joe's accepting attitude has much to do with him being able to date other women, as unlike some Muslim men from strict cultures, it has meant that he has had to learn that women have their own lives to lead. 'He told me that he understood that my career is important and that I am passionate about my work.'

These are some of the key things that Amna wants to hear from a man, because in the past, she felt that Muslim men wanted to try to change her and have her slow down with her work. However, after getting to know Joe for a period of time, Amna realised that they were not automatically compatible.

'I don't know that I am that convinced about my convert theory anymore.'

Even if her views may now have softened, Amna says she does not regret giving her parents advance notice of her opinion on men. By so doing, she was being true to her dive-in-headfirst attitude to life.

She readily admits that she is less tolerant these days of her parents' views on relationships. Her father came to Australia at the age of 24; her mother when she was three. In her opinion, both have had plenty of time to adjust to life in Australia and to shift their attitudes.

But for a long time, Amna's father had what she called the 'survivor migrant mentality'. Having arrived in Australia with very little, life for Bassam was all about getting a job, making money and paying his family's bills.

Amna believes that her father was heavily burdened

socially and economically by moving to Australia and building a new life for himself and his family—an aspect of migration that is little discussed. Her father was so focused on putting food on the table for his family, she says he had little time for much else when Amna and her brothers and sisters were growing up. As the eldest of six children, Amna was expected to help out.

All her life it has been her father's approval Amna has sought. Football was just one of those battlefronts. It is difficult for her to fathom when she reflects on it now, but her father had never wanted her to go to university. 'What's that going to achieve?' he had asked.

She also finds it difficult to understand her father's contradictory position on some matters. For instance, he opposed her foray into the world of woman's football, and yet he has been far more accepting of her work commitments outside of traditional hours.

'He thinks with work that I'm obligated, and argues far less when I spend long periods of time away from home for that. In his mind, if it's a work thing, it's different.'

In the same way as she has been determined to pursue her football dream, Amna attended university, and her father eventually came around to the idea that young women like her could continue with their education while at the same time supporting their family.

After six years of training dozens of girls, both Muslim and non-Muslim, and playing scores of matches, her father finally agreed to attend one of her team's end-of-season presentation nights. At last Bassam would get a glimpse inside his daughter's sporting world. He had never turned up to a single game, despite promising many times that he would.

Over the years, however, Bassam had become gradually more accustomed to the comings and goings of 'Amna's girls' when they visited his house during football season. While her father was always welcoming, he had constantly complained that Amna was giving too much time to her football and not enough to her family.

'The girls had become like family,' Amna explains.

As Amna's public profile grew, however, and as she received recognition—including in the media—for the positive contribution she was making to the community, Bassam had increasingly become aware of her achievements and was now ready to show her his support in public.

Earlier on the day of the presentation, Amna's nerves were focused entirely on her father. She grew anxious that he would change his mind and be a no-show. After checking in with her mother, she had been reassured that he was coming and things would go to plan.

'I knew it was a significant moment when he arrived,' Amna recalls, after her parents walked into the reception hall and took their place at her table.

As Amna took to the stage to host the presentation, she felt confident in her role.

Throughout the night—and entirely unprompted—a steady stream of women sought out Amna's father to sing her praises.

'You should be proud of your daughter,' said a businesswoman with a high profile, who had provided sponsorship for Amna's team.

When the formalities were finally out of the way, Amna pulled her father on to the dance floor. Nothing was going to stop her from being her usual spontaneous self.

As the music blared in the background and the centre of the hall filled with excited young women keen to celebrate their year of hard work on the sports field, it was obvious to onlookers that Bassam was no dancer. Not that it mattered, because this time he took the lead.

Tightly wrapping his arms around Amna, he buried his face—now wet with tears—into her shoulder.

Afterword

In bringing this book together, I have learned something new from each and every one of the women I interviewed—not only about Islam, but also about myself as a Muslim.

I now have a deeper understanding of how Islam is lived through many different cultural lenses, and that this can have a dramatic impact on one's experiences. Perhaps Muslims could do more to understand these differences about each other, as some do not feel they are represented in the prevailing dominant Sunni/Middle Eastern narrative of being a Muslim in Australia.

I hope this book challenged you, too, to better understand that the Muslim community in Australia, so often portrayed as homogenous, comes in all shapes and sizes.

Despite our differences, one thing is clearer to me, now more than ever before: that the five pillars of Islam—believing in the one God, fasting, praying, going to Mecca and giving to charity—guide and sustain a Muslim no matter where they come from or live in the world.

Even so, I've also realised how easy it is for us second generation Muslims—and children of migrants to Australia in general, for that matter—to forget just how difficult it would have been to move to another country for a new life, leaving your family behind. Many arrived with just a suitcase to their name.

So, to the parents of all of the women I interviewed—and the many others like them—this book pays tribute to you too. Many have come to Australia from countries with entrenched ways of living, rooted in long tradition. It would have been easier for them to resist change. But in many ways, they have tried to embrace it and, in so doing, have given their children opportunities they would never have had in their home countries. This has happened in an evolutionary way, allowing new ideas to take shape, while maintaining the essence of some older practices.

I think my dad, Anwar Jamal, was ahead of the times for his lack of adherence to gender and cultural stereotypes in terms of what I would do with my life. When I was in primary school, I had some homework about the age-old question: what do you want to be when you grow up? I remember telling him that I wanted to be a princess—and how offended he was by the notion. 'Say you want to be a writer,' he suggested.

While I do not consider myself a writer in the traditional sense, as it is not my full-time occupation, I like asking people questions, hearing their stories and sometimes writing about them—a privilege that has helped me to better understand the world.

Acknowledgements

This book would not have been possible without the support of Allen & Unwin's Consultant Publisher, Richard Walsh.

Richard, you pushed me when I needed it, which was most of the time, and never gave up on me or this book. More than anything, thank you for being interested in stories about Australian women, particularly those who are Muslim and about the issues affecting them that go beyond the headlines. Australia needs more thinkers like you.

In the same way you believed in me, so too did my family, especially my sisters Hanadi and Nahida, and brothers Kamal and Abdul Karim. I never thought I would say this, but thanks for all the arguments over the dinner table about everything in the news. It's made me the curious person I am today. As Mum always told us, 'You're the best.'

Thanks must also go to Allen & Unwin's Elizabeth Weiss and Rebecca Allen, who helped me bring the book to life.

And finally, a special note of gratitude to Widyan Fares, who agreed to feature on the cover. Widyan has worked as a news journalist and became one of the first reporters in a hijab to appear on Australian national television. She is a PhD candidate at the University of Sydney and, in her spare time, models fashion for Muslim women.